Outsourcing of Core Legal Service Functions

How to Capitalise on Opportunities for Law Firms

Editor
Norman K Clark

Managing director
Sian O'Neill

Outsourcing of Core Legal Service Functions: How to Capitalise on Opportunities for Law Firms
is published by

Globe Law and Business Ltd
3 Mylor Close
Horsell
Woking
Surrey GU21 4DD
United Kingdom
Tel: +44 20 3745 4770
www.globelawandbusiness.com

Outsourcing of Core Legal Service Functions: How to Capitalise on Opportunities for Law Firms

ISBN 9781787424104
EPUB ISBN 9781787424111
Adobe PDF ISBN 9781787424128
Mobi ISBN 9781787424135

Table of contents

I. The business case for the outsourcing of core legal service functions

Norman K Clark
Fernando Moreno
Walker Clark LLC[1]

1. Introduction

Market-driven disruption of the competition for legal services, accelerated by the economic uncertainties of the COVID-19 pandemic, is causing many traditional law firms, of all sizes and practice specialties worldwide, to take a closer look at the strategic business case for outsourcing internal legal service and support functions that previously had been assumed to be managed best in-house. Outsourcing of these traditionally internal functions is becoming increasingly important for smaller firms.[2]

Why should a law firm consider shifting an essential function in the production and delivery of a legal service – what we describe as a core legal service function – to an outside vendor? As this report examines in depth three areas of outsourced legal process operations – patent research and analysis, cybersecurity and large-scale document review – a strong theme emerges: sustainable profitability, which is the ability to deliver high-quality legal services, often in volume, at a price that is competitive but also profitable.[3] Outsourcing of a core legal service function can have not only positive effects on the main forces that drive and determine the profitability of a practice group or an entire law firm, but can also yield two advantages that can be compelling: lowering the operating cost of the production of a legal service; and raising the level of quality.

2. What should be outsourced?

As the subsequent chapters of this Special Report emphasise, a well-informed outsourcing decision requires more than a superficial understanding of the processes by which a supplier produces a service that is delivered to a law firm and of some of the issues that the vendors must manage in order to deliver a consistently high-quality, cost-effective product or service. In most jurisdictions, almost any legal process, just like almost any administrative function, can be outsourced, even the formulation of legal advice or the presentation of a legal opinion (consistent, of course, with local regulations on the unauthorised practice of law). This Special Report focuses on three types of outsourced core legal services functions, each one of which is at the heart of the way in which law firms practise their profession and deliver expert services and products to clients. Each one of these three areas can serve as a useful case study for the application of the principles and methods that this Special Report recommends to address three critical issues inherent in outsourcing:

- Which core functions will produce the best return on our investment in outsourcing?
- What factors should we consider when selecting an external service provider?
- What risks must we be prepared to manage?

"In most jurisdictions, almost any legal process, just like almost any administrative function, can be outsourced, even the formulation of legal advice or the presentation of a legal opinion (consistent, of course, with local regulations on the unauthorised practice of law)."

3. Sustainable profitability as an intellectual framework for well-informed decisions

Outsourcing core legal functions of a law firm – especially ones that are costly, labour intensive, or prone to errors that require corrective rework – has become an essential consideration for most law firms that want to improve and sustain their profitability in a legal services market that is changing swiftly, often in fundamental ways, and becoming more intensely competitive. Understanding the factors that shape the profitability of legal services – often called the *Six Classic Drivers of law firm profitability*[4] – can help law firm leaders and managers to develop specific, realistic objectives to be obtained from outsourcing a core legal function, as well as manage risks and avoid disappointments. These six factors are:

- Pricing – are you charging a high enough fee?
- Productivity – are your fee-earners utilised fully with billable work?
- Realisation – what percentage of your billable work produced is actually collected?
- Cost management – how efficiently and effectively do you manage operating costs?
- Staff compensation – are your fee earners producing at least as much as they are paid?
- Leverage – is your ratio of work produced by associates to work produced by partners high enough to be profitable?

The impacts of outsourcing a particular core legal function, in terms of its positive effects and risks on each of the six drivers, collectively constitute the business case for, or in some cases against, the decision to outsource. This same analysis can also serve as a highly effective risk management plan for the outsourced function:

- by alerting a law firm's management team to the possible risks in terms of financial performance, professional indemnity and reputation;
- by providing 'early warning signs' that a problem is emerging; and
- by allowing the firm and the vendor to take proactive steps to mitigate the risk when it arises or to avoid its potential consequences altogether.

The authors have observed that the most frequent benefits to profitability that outsourcing of a core legal function can produce are with respect to four of the Six Classic Drivers of profitability:

- staff costs;
- productivity;
- leverage; and
- realisation.

3.1 Lower staff costs

As discussed in subsequent chapters, a well-informed outsourcing of a core legal function can produce positive results, directly or indirectly, for each of the Six Classic Drivers. In most instances, the cost of one full-time equivalent (FTE) of outsourced services can be significantly less than the total cost of having the same services performed by one similarly qualified full-time in-house employee.[5] The benefit that is obvious to most law firms considering outsourcing is to reduce staffing costs, especially at the lawyer level, which are usually the largest single element of the fully-loaded operating cost of a law firm. Fully-loaded operating cost is, essentially, how much it costs a law firm or a practice group to produce one hour of legal services. Even for matters that are not billed at an hourly rate, fully-loaded operating cost remains the most accurate and reliable baseline measurement for managing profitability. This is the case in most legal services markets in the world, especially where the practice areas and service lines of some law firms are being squeezed between higher price sensitivity and fiercer competition, which lowers revenue and increases operating costs, especially in lawyer and staff compensation and benefits.[6]

3.2 Improved productivity

One frequently overlooked potential benefit of outsourcing core legal functions that are typically performed by lawyers and highly skilled paralegals is the potential positive impact on the productivity of the people whose work is outsourced.

Productivity is not limited only to the number of hours that produce or contribute to the production of billable work. The value of the work produced – measured in collected fees – should also be considered. By shifting lawyer and paralegal time and effort from the outsourced tasks to higher-value ones, in terms of their fee potential, the outsourcing can produce a substantially higher fee yield per fee-earner hour. Sometimes this effect on overall profitability can be greater than any potential net savings in salaries and benefits which could result from eliminating redundancies.

3.3 Improved leverage and greater partner fee productivity

The concept of leverage is changing in law firms worldwide.

The traditional definition of leverage was expressed in terms of staffing ratios, such as the ratio of the number of associates to the number of partners. A common assumption – actually more of a rebuttable presumption – has been that a ratio of four associates to one partner was usually profitable, especially with fixed-fee work.[7] This is consistent with the general rule that legal work should be delegated down to the least expensive person who can do it competently. Delegation also has the added benefit of freeing partner time for higher-value activities,

"In most instances, the cost of one full-time equivalent (FTE) of outsourced services can be significantly less than the total cost of having the same services performed by one similarly qualified full-time in-house employee."

such as higher-priced legal services that require a partner's expertise and personal attention, or business development.[8]

The more useful concept in today's law firm, however, is workflow leverage, which measures the ratio of work performed, usually measured in 'billable' hours, rather than just staffing ratios. Workflow leverage provides a more accurate picture of how the work of a law firm actually flows and is performed. This is more useful for purposes of identifying opportunities to improve leverage than staffing ratios because many law firms typically under-delegate work. There are various reasons – and in some cases weak excuses – for low workflow leverage, the most common ones being the assumption – sometimes erroneous but often accurate – by partners that 'there is no one competent to do this work' or that 'it is quicker and easier just to do it myself'. Low workflow leverage, when examined, can be a strong diagnostic indicator of opportunities to make substantial and lasting improvements in profitability.

How does outsourcing affect leverage? The simple, but frequently overlooked, answer is that it can provide another dimension and destination for delegated work (ie, out of the firm). Because the cost of most outsourced core legal functions is less than the fully-loaded operating cost of performing these functions in-house – even at the least expensive level of staff that is competent to do the work – it can extend workflow leverage dramatically, with a resulting improvement in profitability.

3.4 Quality and realisation

Realisation describes how much of a firm's labour is realised in the form of cash receipts. Does every hour of billable work produced ultimately result in an hour's worth of fee revenue? Close attention to realisation rates is, for most law firms, the most powerful way to improve the profitability of a practice without any significant increase in staff or operating costs. Every pound that a law firm does not have to write off is almost pure profit.[9]

Analyses of fee write-offs and write-downs, both before and after invoicing, will usually reveal that defects in quality assurance constitute a leading reason for this lost revenue.[10] Part of the attractiveness of outsourcing large-volume tasks – with their very large potential for errors – is that the primary responsibility for quality assurance is also outsourced to an organisation that is better structured for, and more experienced in, the high levels of accuracy and reliability that are required to meet customer expectations the first time and every time. This is a theme that runs through the next three chapters. In some instances, the reductions in fee adjustments and write-offs, and the resulting increase in revenue, by themselves can substantially offset the costs of outsourcing the function.

4. Selecting a core legal function for outsourcing

Which functions are the best candidates for outsourcing? We recommend a relatively simple cost-based and risk-based approach to start the analysis.

- **Map the process.** A simple flow chart, which identifies the major steps or action in the performance of the function, is usually adequate.
- **Estimate the fully-loaded operating cost of each step that is currently performed in-house.** In most instances, a fully-loaded operating cost per fee-earner hour of work and the average number of fee-earner hours required to perform the task (based on time and billing records) will provide an estimate that is accurate and reliable enough to identify the specific tasks, functions and actions that cost the most and, therefore, bite most deeply into the profits of the firm or practice group.
- **Assess the risks in each step.** What is the probability of error? If an error is made, what is the relative severity of the reasonably foreseeable losses to the firm in terms of unbillable work, fee write-offs, client dissatisfaction, professional liability and harm to reputation?

This evaluation can produce a matrix (Table 1) that summarises the relative cost and risk potential of each of the major steps.

Table 1. Cost and risk analysis

Step	Fully-loaded operating cost/hour	Average hours	Estimated cost of each step	Probability of errors	Relative severity of an error
1	£305	0.5	£ 152.50	15.5%	low
2	£155	3.3	£ 511.50	41.7%	moderate
3	£305	1.0	£ 305.00	12.5%	moderate
4	£190	1.2	£ 228.00	39.6%	high
5	£245	0.5	£ 122.50	49.5%	low
6	£400	1.5	£ 600.00	8.0%	high
7	£400	0.5	£ 200.00	3.2%	high
Total		**8.50**	**£2,119.50**		

There is no universal formula to decide which of the steps in the above example are the best candidates for outsourcing. The selection should depend on the underlying objectives and desired results that the firm wants to achieve in terms of lower operating cost, lower quality-related risk or both. This analysis can also help a law firm decide whether to outsource an entire function – from start to finish – or only selected parts. Each of the steps in the above example appears to offer an opportunity.

- If your goal is to free higher-priced fee earners to perform other functions, Steps 6, 7, 3 and 1, in that order, would appear to offer significant savings (£1,257.50 in the value of high-end fee-earner time, or 59.30%) if they can be outsourced for a lower cost.
- If your goal is to delegate otherwise 'billable' hours outside the firm, freeing up more time for other work, then Step 3, with an average of 3.3 hours, would appear to be the most tempting target for a partial outsourcing of the function.
- If your goal is better risk management by outsourcing a step, as well as the responsibility for quality assurance, to an external service provider, then Steps 5, 4 and 2, in that order, currently involve the highest probability of errors and unproductive rework to correct them. These steps are currently producing

"The old paradigm of service quality in legal services, which dominated the legal services industry and client expectations before 2000, offered a client three possible service advantages – low price, fast delivery and high professional quality – but required the client to settle for only two of the three."

low realisation rates and are possibly losing money because of the relatively high error rates.
- Alternatively, if you want to reduce the firm's overall exposure to the most serious consequences of inadequate in-house quality assurance, Steps 4, 6 and 7 would be the most likely targets. Step 4 is especially troublesome because it has a relatively high probability of error (39.6%) with a relatively high severity of the possible risk, in terms of potential harm. In other words, in more than one-third of the cases where Step 4 is performed, mistakes are made with the highest relative level of severity of potential harm.

5. Outsourcing as a source of competitive advantage

Profitability is not the only consideration for outsourcing of a core legal function, however. Law firms should also consider the extent to which outsourcing of a core legal function will enable them to offer superior quality services, especially in price-sensitive service lines and industry sectors, at highly competitive low prices, but still at a reasonable level of profit for the overall service that is delivered by the firm.

The old paradigm of service quality in legal services, which dominated the legal services industry and client expectations before 2000, offered a client three possible service advantages – low price, fast delivery and high professional quality – but required the client to settle for only two of the three:

- The client could have the service at a low price and with fast delivery, but it would not be with high professional quality; or
- The client could have the service quickly, and with high professional quality, but it would not be at a low price; or
- The client could have the service with high professional quality and at a low price, but it would not be fast.

Traditional law firms forced this three-pronged dilemma on clients because most of them were unable, under the prevailing operational paradigms of the time, to manage all three. Today, however, sophisticated consumers of legal services demand all three: high professional quality delivered quickly and at a low cost. Moreover, the entry of non-traditional professional service providers into the legal services industry, as well as the adoption by progressive law firms of total quality management concepts, tools and methods, have made all three possible. Law firms that still insist that they can deliver only the old 'choose only two' model are being swept aside and, in our opinion, probably will not survive the next 10 years unless they make some fundamental changes.

Well-informed, strategically driven outsourcing of core legal functions to expert external service providers can enable law firms and practice groups to deliver 'all three' while not only sustaining reasonable levels of profitability but actually improving them.

The case studies in the next three chapters examine in-depth how external service providers perform important core legal functions in three areas: patent research and analysis; information security; and high-volume document review in support of litigation. The authors of these chapters were invited by the editors based on their experience, insight and success in their respective service areas. Although their areas of expertise and perspectives are different, each one presents a detailed exposition of the services they offer, the fundamental strengths of each outsourcing model, and the conditions for a successful selection of an external service provider and/or the successful management of the outsourcing relationship.

Notes

1 Walker Clark LLC is an international legal management consultancy, based in the United States with team members also in Europe and Latin America. Founded in 2002, the firm's practice specialises in strategic, operational and performance advice and support to law firms, corporate and government legal departments, and professional services networks worldwide.

2 The definitions of, and differences between, small, midsize and large firms are slippery concepts, not easily locked into numbers of partners, fee earners or staff. They are also determined to a large extent by the prevailing size of law firms in any given market and by clients' expectations of expertise and service-delivery capabilities. For example, the largest law firm in a jurisdiction might have 20 lawyers – 'small' by global standards but 'large' in terms of the expectations of its clients.
For the purpose of consistency in this Special Report, however, the editors and authors propose that, except where noted otherwise, a 'small' law firm is one with fewer than 50 lawyers, a 'midsize' law firm has between 50 and 150 lawyers and a 'large' law firm has more than 150 lawyers. This classification reflects our experience and observations that when most, but certainly not all, law firms pass the thresholds of 20, 50 and 150 lawyers, the management requirements measured by partner time and operating costs per fee earner tend to change disproportionately, usually upward in what we would describe as a 'quantum jump'. Our experience, observations and research suggest, therefore, that at least 98.5% of the world's law firms would fit into these classifications of 'small' and 'midsize'.

3 See Norman Clark and Lisa Walker Johnson, *Sustainable Profitability in a Disrupted Legal Market* (London: Globe Law and Business, 2019) for a detailed analysis of the Six Classic Drivers of law firm profitability in the changing competitive environment of the legal services industry.

4 See, *Sustainable Profitability*, *op cit*, pp13–23 for an overview of the Six Classic Drivers and the impact of each one on the ability of a law firm to improve and sustain satisfactory levels of profitability.

5 For example, the authors have observed that the total cost for one FTE of outsourced patent research and analysis services can be, depending on the market in which the contracting law firm is located, between 40% and 60% of the same services performed by a similarly qualified in-house employee, with the 'similarly qualified' requirement being a serious limitation for some law firms.
In short, we have observed a substantial and, we suspect, possibly irreversible flow of expertise from traditional law firms to focused external providers of these services.

6 Fully-loaded operating cost usually is the total of the operating costs and the compensation and benefits paid to non-owner lawyers and staff, excluding capitalised expenses. When divided by the number of produced 'billable' hours (ie, hours that produce billable work, whether billed on an hourly rate or other non-hourly basis), this measurement provides a reasonably accurate 'break-even point' for a legal product or service.
It is a simple measurement, easily within the capability of any law firm, even the smallest one, but it remains largely unknown or ignored. In a few cases in the authors' experience, the managing partners of law firms have declined to report it, even to equity partners or owners, for fear that it could be internally divisive among partners in different practice areas or groups. Nonetheless, even if the numbers are not as complete or as precise as one would like, every law firm needs to know its break-even point for every service or product they deliver. Without this information, fee quotations are little more than hopeful guesswork, see *Sustainable Profitability*, *op cit*, p27.

7 This 4-to-1 ratio is subject to considerable adjustment depending on the level of experience,

expertise or sophistication required by the nature of the matters, such as when clients expect that substantially all the work will be performed by a partner. There also appears to be an upper limit to profitable delegation. The authors have observed that once a staffing ratio exceeds 6-to-1, there is a proportionately increased incidence of errors and unbillable rework due to inadequate supervision and quality control by supervising partners. Partners simply do not have the time to supervise the output of more than six associates, especially when advances in information technology is substantially increasing the output capabilities of each associate. One of the first diagnostic indicators of an unmanageable leverage level is a steady decline in the billing realisation rate for the practice group, as the time recorded to correct mistakes usually cannot be billed, much less collected.

8 In the authors' experience and observations, which include a limited number of analyses of time records in various law firms in different legal markets, it appears that the average return on investment in one hour of partner time devoted to developing new instructions and matters from existing clients is substantially higher than from producing one hour of billable work at that partner's standard hourly rate. On average, one hour of partner time spent in business development with existing clients can produce the equivalent of between eight and 16 hours of new billable work for the firm. The variation within the range tends to be practice-area specific. Nonetheless, if a partner who usually records 1,500 hours of billable work per year can delegate 10% of those hours to an associate and devote those 150 hours to business development with existing clients, the 150 'newly available' hours should produce, at a mid-range 12-to-1 return on investment, approximately 1,800 hours of new work. Even if all this work is performed and billed at an associate's lower hourly rate, the revenue increase is substantial.

9 For a detailed explanation of the role of realisation in improving and sustaining profitability, see *Sustainable Profitability*, *op cit*, pp47–56.

10 In one firm that Walker Clark LLC advised on quality assurance matters, we found that almost 70% of the write-downs and write-offs were directly linked to unbillable time needed to correct errors, most of which should have and could have been prevented by adequate quality assurance protocols and procedures. This resulted not only in fees that could not be billed to the client, but also in opportunity costs arising from the unavailability of the 'repair crew' to do other higher-value legal work. Document-intensive processes are particularly susceptible to errors. Rather than invest unbillable time in fixing mistakes once they are discovered, the better practice is to identify the most common causes of errors and reduce their occurrence or even eliminate them altogether.

II. Patent drafting, research and analysis

Tushar Gupta
Gaurav Khandelwal
Intricate Research[1]

1. A few preliminary questions

- Has your firm decided to enter a new practice area?
- Do you want to expand the existing business line?
- Are you hampered by conventional techniques?
- Do you want to enhance the quality of your service?
- Are you thinking of providing value-added services or innovations to the existing service offerings to the end client?
- Do you want to spend your quality time on client engagement rather than working on projects and deliverables?
- Is employing fixed human resources a challenge for you?
- Do you lack the requisite technical expertise?
- Are you unable to devote your time to core functions?
- Are you shocked to learn that your firm is collecting only 75% of the fees that you have agreed with your clients and want to know what your firm can do to raise this rate to 100%?

2. Not just an efficient tool, but also a smart one

> *If you deprive yourself of outsourcing and your competitors do not, you're putting yourself out of business.*
>
> Lee Kuan Yew
> Former Prime Minister of Singapore

In today's world, intellectual property (IP) outsourcing is not just an efficient option but also a smart one. The global knowledge process outsourcing market is expected to grow at a compound annual growth rate (CAGR) of ~17.6% during the 2016–2025 period, to reach US$124.29 billion in 2025, with India being one of the leading outsourcing destinations. Intellectual Property Research has been very much part of this increasing market, which can be attributed to the fact that large technology companies such as Microsoft, Apple, Google and Qualcomm are outsourcing their IP work to Indian service providers. It should be noted that, apart from the big corporates, academic institutions, small and medium-sized enterprises, and law firms have started recognising the importance of IP outsourcing and have begun to explore this path. Within the IP field, patent service is an area that has not been explored completely for outsourcing. It cannot be said that companies and law firms have not tried outsourcing their patent work, but they are far from leveraging the true potential of patent service outsourcing. Patent service providers can support clients with various functions ranging from search, analysis, proofreading, drafting, patent filing, renewals, and portfolio management through to research and development.

"In today's world, intellectual property (IP) outsourcing is not just an efficient option but also a smart one."

Figure 1. Key patent services

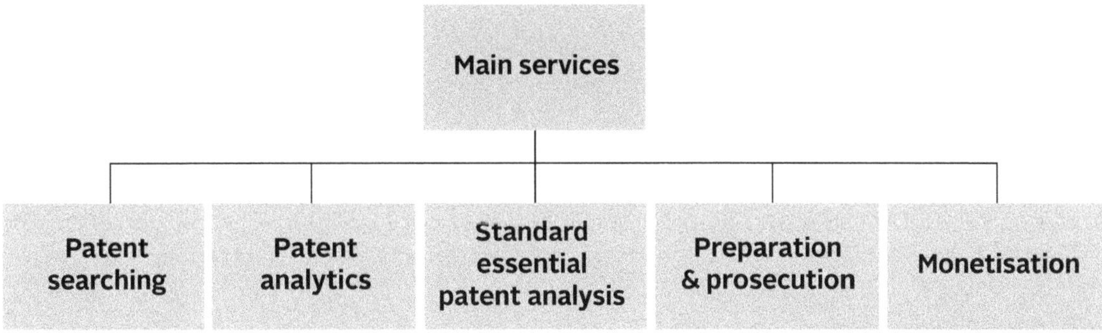

3. Which patent services can be outsourced?
To get more insight into patent outsourcing, it is essential to first go through the key patent services which can be outsourced. Broadly speaking, the patent services can be classified as shown in Figure 1 above.

These are the five broad service headings under which there are a number of patent services that can be outsourced.

3.1 Patent searching

a) Patentability search/pre-filing search (patent novelty search)
A patentability search helps to identify relevant prior arts at the initial stages of IP creation. It enables clients to make informed decisions about patent drafting and filing strategies and, in turn, reduces patent prosecution cost and time.

The advantages of outsourcing this service: Patentability searches will be performed by experts who will comprehensively search every aspect of an invention to find out the closest prior art (whether in patents or non-patent literature) and provide a well-informed patentability opinion.

b) Invalidity/validity search

Patent invalidity/validity searches are conducted to either validate the claims of a patent or to invalidate one or more claims of a competitor's patent. An invalidity or opposition search is conducted to identify patent and non-patent documents which may impact the claims of a specific patent. This can help block patents and establish the strength of a patent portfolio, which may be useful for licensing or company acquisition.

The advantages of outsourcing this service: The invalidity/validity searches will be performed by experts who will specifically focus on:

- having an accurate understanding of the technology of the patent and scope of the claims;
- accurately defining the novel aspect of the patent based on the specifications and file history; and
- validating that the identified prior art serves as a valid prior art under respective regional laws, for example, 35 USC Sections 102–103 for the United States and Articles 54 and 56 of the European Patent Convention.

Their search strategy will be comprehensive and cover a variety of aspects including keywords/concepts-based searching, patent classification-based searching (eg, CPC,[2] IPC,[3] USPC,[4] FI,[5] F-Term[6] based searching), assignee and inventors-based searching, citation search/spider searching and semantic searching.

c) Freedom-to-operate/clearance search

Freedom to operate (FTO) refers to whether it is commercially safe to launch a product in a given country without inadvertently stepping onto the claimed technology of someone's patents. The FTO/clearance search identifies the issued or pending patents that may be a threat to the product or process that you wish to market.

An FTO search should be carried out as early as possible, preferably at the time of conceptualisation of the product or technology. There may be cases where at the time of conceptualisation of the product its features are not well defined, but gradually as the work on the actual product begins, the key product features start to form a structure and eventually with time and progress become finalised. Even in this case, it is mandatory to conduct an FTO study before you begin the commercialisation of your product or technology. Conducting a timely FTO study offers two key benefits:

- it avoids unnecessary costs and wasted allocation of resources; and
- it reduces the risk of costly and time-consuming future litigation, which may damage the brand image.

The advantages of outsourcing this service: Generally, experienced patent service providers assist clients in FTO clearance searches for various jurisdictions across the globe on a variety of technology domains. The patent service provider will conduct a thorough search and deliver a report that includes an exhaustive list of potentially harmful patents. The patent service provider prepares mapping between the claims of these patents and the key features of the product that is to be launched commercially. Further, the patent service provider gives valuable information about the legal status of the patents, especially applications that are in the prosecution stage.

d) State of the Art search

A State of the Art search provides up-to-date information about progress in a specific technical field. It is a survey that takes a broad look at everything that has been done (everything disclosed to the public, including patent and non-patent literature) in a given technology area. For a company that is currently active in a particular field, the results of a State of the Art search can provide guidance showing how to design around the current art.

"An FTO search should be carried out as early as possible, preferably at the time of conceptualisation of the product or technology."

The advantages of outsourcing this service: By providing a State of the Art search, the patent service provider allows its clients to spot new market entrants and close competition, and to identify new technological trends.

3.2 Patent analytics

There are range of analytics services based on in-depth analysis of patent and market data and trends.

a) Patent landscape

Patent landscape provides a snapshot of the patent situation of a particular technology or in a company of interest. Apart from providing a bird's-eye view, the landscape report outlines the key features of the particular technology area of interest. The report provides an analysis of patent data that reveals business, scientific and technological trends. Landscape reports typically focus on a single industry, technology or geographic region. The landscape report includes interactive widgets with easy-to-understand analyses.

The advantages of outsourcing this service: Generally, an experienced patent service provider will conduct an in-depth analysis to ascertain the existing technology and future market trends while understanding the client's objective of getting the patent landscape study conducted. The patent service provider will provide a comprehensive report that will help in identifying:

- innovation focus of companies, industries and countries;
- technology leaders and their IP strategies;
- potential white spaces/gap analysis in a technology domain/patent portfolio;
- technological positioning of companies;
- licensing, investment, joint venture, and merger and acquisition opportunities;
- entry or exit strategy from a market;
- competitors' research and development strategy;
- unique selling points of companies; and
- strengths and weaknesses of patent portfolios.

b) Market intelligence

This service area provides a current market scenario of a particular technology area. It helps the clients to understand the current market scenario and the future scope of development while entering a new technology domain or geographical region.

The advantages of outsourcing this service: A patent service provider will gather data from various sources/databases to provide the client with the big picture and an in-depth analysis of a technology market.

"By providing a State of the Art search, the patent service provider allows its clients to spot new market entrants and close competition, and to identify new technological trends."

Generally, an expert service provider will provide a detailed study which outlines key market trends, valuable products, and major players and their strategies. The patent service provider will prepare competitor intelligence reports to help the clients understand innovation focus, market penetration strategy and the development plans of their competitors.

c) Competitor monitoring

Competitor monitoring involves a comprehensive study of a competitor's patent portfolio and patenting strategy. Based on the client's requirements, competitor monitoring may be a one-time analysis of a competitor's patent portfolio or a periodic patent watch.

This can include portfolio analysis and patent mining services, which analyses from various viewpoints a patent portfolio held by a corporation or an individual. Generally, this service is carried out in order to examine and segment the patent portfolio of a competitor in a manner that helps develop a better understanding of the competitor's overall strategy. However, this service can be performed to understand one's own portfolio and, based on that, make informed decisions.

The advantages of outsourcing this service: As a part of this service, the patent service provider will provide a detailed report including the competitor's SWOT (strengths, weaknesses, opportunities, threats) analysis, segmentation of the competitor's patent portfolio (based on developed taxonomy), and identification of key patents. Further, the in-depth analysis performed by the service provider would be extremely useful in understanding the competitor's strategies for mergers and acquisitions, research and development, and its key innovators or inventors. Some patent service providers have an in-house proprietary patent ranking tool which takes into consideration various qualitative and quantitative parameters to rank and segment the patent portfolio.

d) Patent watch and monitoring

This service involves regular monitoring and tracking of competitors' patents. The newly published patent applications and issued patents in the targeted technology are monitored to stay abreast of technical developments in the field of interest. The watch service helps in analysing concerned patents in the technology field to identify business opportunities and threats.

The advantages of outsourcing this service: As a part of this service, the patent service provider regularly and periodically tracks the new pending patent applications, newly granted patents, new abandoned or expired patents, legal status change, and new litigations to enable the client to stay ahead of its competitors and have a forward-looking approach.

e) Patent summary and expert patent analysis

In a patent summary analysis, a particular patent is analysed to determine its technical scope, as well as to identify the advantages of the patented technology and the market applicability of the innovation. This service helps the client to be aware of the patented technology and understand its features. The analysis involves assessment of the patent quality based on various parameters. This service can be used to identify high-quality assets in a patent portfolio. Clients may utilise this service for patent portfolio pruning and identifying the quality of a patent portfolio. The service may also act as a pre-screening step for identifying potential patents for evidence-of-use analysis.

The advantages of outsourcing this service: The patent service provider performs an analysis of a patent under consideration. The analysis encompasses the separate sections discussing problems in prior art, current technical solutions, and a summary of the advantages of the invention, market applicability of the patented technology, impact of the invention, as well as a list of companies which can be

"Standard mapping services involve the analysis of technology standards and patent claims to identify overlap between the two."

potential licensees of the patented technology. The analysis can be tweaked based on specific client requirements.

3.3 Standard Essential Patent (SEP) analysis

SEP analysis consists of two key services: standard mapping and SEP verification.

a) Standard mapping

Standard mapping services involve the analysis of technology standards and patent claims to identify overlap between the two. If a patent is found to be essential to a technology standard, it can drastically increase the value of the patent. If one misses out on identifying all the relevant standard essential patents while implementing a technology, one may then be exposed to patent infringement litigation and suffer huge financial loss. Therefore, the standard mapping service is very important for both the patent licensee and licensor.

b) SEP verification

In this service, the essentiality of standard-declared patents is analysed. Based on the extent of overlap between the claims and the declared standard's features or sections, a determination is made about whether the patent is essential or related to the declared standard.

The advantages of outsourcing SEP services: This service needs to be outsourced to a patent service provider who has a highly qualified and experienced team. The team should have well-qualified engineers with expertise in a wide range of technology standards developed by various standard setting organisations (SSOs) – eg, IEEE, 3GPP, ETSI, MPEG and ITU. They should have expertise in working on patent to standard mapping for advanced technologies, such as telecommunications (UMTS, LTE, 5G, Wi-Fi, etc) and video codec (H.264, H.265, VP8, VP9, etc).

3.4 Preparation and prosecution

a) Patent drafting

Patent drafting is the art of techno-legal writing to encompass different features of an invention in written form. Different jurisdictions have different requirements and, therefore, require a different drafting style.

The advantages of outsourcing this service: This service needs to be outsourced to an experienced patent service provider who will follow a comprehensive approach to cover all aspects of an invention, including current and future designs and applications, ensuring complete

"Patent drafting is the art of techno-legal writing to encompass different features of an invention in written form. Different jurisdictions have different requirements and, therefore, require a different drafting style."

protection. While drafting the claims, the service provider should not only focus on getting the drafted patent granted, but also keep in mind the commercial value of the invention. The service provider should draft an application for the invention by working hand-in-hand with the inventors to understand the nature of the invention and help clarify novel features of the invention to the patent office. The patent specifications must be drafted such that it conforms to the standards and requirements of the jurisdiction where the client plans to file the application.

b) Patent filing
Patent filing is a complex procedure which requires submitting various forms in a specified format within strict timelines as specified by the patent office.

The advantages of outsourcing this service: This service needs to be outsourced to a service provider who has a team of patent agents and patent attorneys with vast experience in patent filings and can consult on the best filing strategy matching the client's business strategy. The service provider should assist the clients in every step of the patent prosecution starting from patent application filing to the grant of the application. The service provider should help the clients at every step of patent filing(s) in government patent offices across the globe.

c) Patent illustrations and drawings
As the saying goes, "A picture is worth a thousand words". Patent drawings play a significant role in the precise understanding of an invention. Drawings are an essential part of a patent application. Therefore, it is important to prepare patent drawings which provide a clear and accurate representation of the invention as well as comply with the rules and regulations of the patent office.

The advantages of outsourcing this service: This service needs to be outsourced to a service provider who has a team of draftsmen with experience in creating drawings for patents filed in all the major jurisdictions. For the service provider, the quality of the drawings should be paramount. The service provider should have access to the most advanced software tools for preparing the patent drawings in different file formats as per the client's requirements.

d) Office action response (pre-grant prosecution)
Patent prosecution refers to the interaction between applicants and the patent office with regard to an application or a patent. In patent law, an office action is a document written by a patent examiner in response to a patent application after the examiner has examined the application. The office action cites prior art and gives reasons why the examiner has allowed, or approved, the applicant's claims, and/or

"Patent landscape provides a snapshot of the patent situation of a particular technology or in a company of interest. Apart from providing a bird's-eye view, the landscape report outlines the key features of the particular technology area of interest. The report provides an analysis of patent data that reveals business, scientific and technological trends."

rejected the claims. In response to the office action, an office action response is given by the applicant of a patent to the patent authority during the prosecution of the patent application. A person who responds to an office action should be aware of techno-legal language as he or she would be amending a part of the objected claim elements or arguing on the objections raised by the patent examiner. Responding to office actions is as much an art as it is a science.

The advantages of outsourcing this service: It is always best to outsource the work of office action response to the patent service provider who had initially drafted the patent as he or she would be the techno-legal person who is most aware of every aspect of the invention. Otherwise, if the same service provider is not available, try to find a provider who is able to deal with both patent applications and office action responses. The patent service provider should not draft a short-sighted response merely to overcome the rejections or objections of the examiner, as it could have devastating effects on the eventually granted patent. The response must possess logic and analytical reasoning to broadly interpret and set aside the objection raised in the office action. The response has to be holistic and comprehensive in nature. It should be drafted from the viewpoint that it does not just get the patent granted but also gets the patent granted in a form that makes the patent commercially most valuable and legally strong.

e) Pre-grant opposition (pre-grant prosecution)

Under the pre-grant opposition, any person or third party or government (or authority) may challenge the application for grant of a patent and inform the patent office of the opposition against the grant of a patent after the application for a patent has been published but before the grant of a patent. Pre-grant opposition acts as a defence to confirm the validity of the patent application (before the patent is granted). Furthermore, for opponents, it is a good opportunity to oppose the grant of an unlawful protective right.

The advantages of outsourcing this service: Where you or your firm is the person or third party who wants to challenge the application, it may be wise to engage an experienced patent service provider, especially in a validity/invalidity service. The service provider will need to conduct a thorough and comprehensive search to identify patent and non-patent documents which may impact the claims of the specific patent application. Further, the service provider may challenge the patent application in contention from a technical or legal standpoint. For example, in many countries the requirements regarding novelty, inventive step, industrial applicability, sufficiency of disclosure and addition of new matter going beyond the original disclosure are grounds for an opposition. Non-compliance with the requirements concerning the exclusions from patentable subject matter also forms part of the grounds for an opposition, while some countries accept an opposition on the grounds that an applicant or patentee is not entitled to the right to a patent, or on other grounds covering all requirements that should be fulfilled to obtain a patent. Therefore, in order to raise the pre-grant opposition on technical or legal grounds, the service provider needs to be well versed in the patent laws of the jurisdiction.

f) Post-grant opposition (post-grant prosecution)
In most countries, post-grant opposition may be filed at any time after the grant of a patent, but before the expiry of a period of one year from the date of grant of the patent. Under the post-grant opposition, any interested person may give notice to the patent authority (in the prescribed format and manner, which vary from jurisdiction to jurisdiction) on the grounds recognised by the patent law of the country. Every country defines the criteria for 'interested person' differently. However, this term generally means an individual who is engaged in, or is promoting, research in the same field as that to which the invention relates or an entity or organisation that has a manufacturing, trading or financial interest in the goods related to the patent product.

The advantages of outsourcing this service: Where you or your firm is the interested person or party who wants to challenge the application, it would be wise to engage an experienced patent service provider, especially in validity/invalidity services, who is also well versed in the patent laws of the particular jurisdiction. The service provider needs to conduct a thorough and comprehensive search to identify patent and non-patent documents which may impact the claims of the specific patent application. Similar to pre-grant opposition, the patent service provider may challenge the granted patent on various technical or legal grounds.

3.5 Monetisation
External patent service providers can help a law firm protect and enhance the return on investment of its clients.

a) Infringement analysis (evidence-of-use analysis)
Infringement analysis, also known as evidence-of-use (EoU) analysis, is performed to safeguard and protect the IP and related interest of the patent holder. Its primary goal is to help patent owners identify potentially infringing products, processes or services in the marketplace. Patent infringement refers to the act of producing, using or distributing a patented product, process, or service for a commercial purpose without the permission of the patent holder. As patent rights are territorial in nature, the definition of infringement

varies by jurisdiction. To determine infringement of a patented technology, it is necessary to understand the scope of the protection and the boundary of the patented technology (the claims section of the patent defines the scope of protection granted to a patent). Besides the identification of potential infringers, EoU analysis can also provide information on the patent's future potential for getting the patented technology licensed or sold.

The advantages of outsourcing this service: This service needs to be outsourced to a patent service provider who is skilled in identifying and going through product literature, including manuals and service documents, and who exercises great care while performing the searches. The ability to interpret and comprehend the literature plays a key role. The service provider helps the client by conducting detailed searches for identifying any products or services that may infringe on the subject patent. The infringement search results in identifying a list of products, services, processes or standards that might be based on the technology of the subject patent. The service provider needs to follow a process that includes preparing a list of top players in the technology area related to the subject patent and then preparing a list of products, which includes searching on the websites of companies and original equipment manufacturers, as well as third-party

"Besides the identification of potential infringers, EoU analysis can also provide information on the patent's future potential for getting the patented technology licensed or sold."

subscriptions and other databases. Once the relevant products are identified, the analysis will be completed by referring to various catalogues, manuals, data sheets, white papers, product reviews, videos, brochures and similar literature to ascertain the infringement. At times the service provider may be required to perform hands-on product testing in order to ascertain infringement. Sometimes, depending on the claims of the patent, another approach may also be taken to see if any of the latest technology standards incorporate the features of the patent. In order to do this, the service provider needs to be experienced in working on different standards (eg, IEEE, 3GPP and MPEG).

While preparing an evidence-of-use chart, the service provider should focus on:

- developing a clear understanding of the target patent and its claim(s) in light of the patent specifications and file history to derive the broadest possible interpretation of the independent claims;
- analysing and creating an exhaustive list of potential infringers;
- doing a thorough search on the identified companies and analysing their product portfolios in order to find the most suitable infringing product; and

"At times the service provider may be required to perform hands-on product testing in order to ascertain infringement."

- performing granular mapping of the target claim elements to the features of the identified product.

It should be noted that evidence of use can be established even when there is not a complete mapping between the claim elements and the features of the product or service. However, with complete and credible claim charts, it becomes relatively straightforward to convey that the infringement exists.

b) Patent valuation

The development of patents is not just essential for innovation, technology growth and competitiveness, these assets can also be leveraged as a financial instrument for source of revenue. The commercialisation and monetisation of IP assets offers a number of credit alternatives for borrowers, especially for businesses which have limited financial resources. Therefore, it is very important to first know the actual valuation of an IP asset, which in turn will have an impact on your company's research and development efforts, strengthen your IP rights, and enhance your revenue. Once you know the worth of your patent, then you will be able to monetise (eg, license, sell or mortgage) it to the right candidate at the right price. A patent valuation study enables a company to achieve its strategic and financial goals.

The advantages of outsourcing this service: This service is best performed when it is outsourced as there are no biases involved. If you conduct the patent valuation in-house, you may face a couple of challenges, such as:

- You might not have the right individuals with the requisite skill set to perform this service (as it is a highly specialised service).
- There might be biases involved. In-house personnel might be influenced or, considering it's their own patent, value it at more than it's worth.

Outsourcing this to the right service provider helps to overcome these two potential obstructions. The service provider assigns a monetary value to your IP asset which lets you unleash its hidden potential. The service provider needs to use a multidisciplinary approach for determining the optimal value of the patent by conducting technical, market or industry evaluations, and financial research. Generally, skilled and experienced service providers have already developed financial models which assist in ascertaining a patent's real value.

c) Broker tie-ups

In order to monetise your IP assets, you should contact a patent brokerage firm. It is difficult for an in-house professional or an in-house team to identify potential licensees directly without external help.

The advantages of outsourcing this service: This service needs to be outsourced to identify the right set of individuals or firms who can understand the value of your asset and pay the right amount of money as per the worth of the patent. Finding potential licensees is a specialised service and requires good industry connections to find the right buyer or licensee of the patented technology. To do this, it is good if you can find the right patent broker. Alternatively, you may choose a patent service provider who has already partnered with a number of patent brokerage firms which have years of experience in monetisation (ie, selling, purchasing and licensing) of patent assets. It is sometimes best to engage the patent service provider who has already conducted the patent analysis (such as EoU chart, or patent valuation) and also has good connections with broker firms. The experienced patent service provider who has a good relationship with patent broker firms, generally creates an attractive marketing package for monetisation of patent assets. Thereafter, the brokerage firms leverage their industry knowledge and experience to identify potential buyers and licensees and generate a good value proposition for the patents to be monetised.

4. Business engagement models

We have already discussed various patent services along with the outsourcing aspects related to each of them. The outsourcing models followed by different organisations provide various benefits. The major objective achieved through outsourcing is cost reduction and improved turnaround time. It also helps organisations leverage knowledge and experience of a patent service provider which will contribute towards the development of a strong IP strategy. The importance of IP outsourcing is reinforced by the fact that many organisations lack the strategy and management expertise required to unlock the value of their IP asset. Moreover, it is not always cost efficient, strategically aligned or sometimes viable to build such expertise in-house.

This is precisely the same logic that drove the outsourcing of IT, which resulted in major efficiency gains. IP outsourcing can convert what is often a reactive, defensively focused cost centre into a proactive, strategically important profit centre. For achieving distinct objectives, different organisations have different engagement models with patent service providers. The business engagement model selected should be convenient, efficient and help the organisation achieve its goals.

An engagement model is a plan that determines the type of collaboration between the organisation (client) and the service provider. Generally, the engagement model should be tailor-made, a one-size-fits-all approach is not suitable. However, there are some well-known, prevalent and successful engagement models that are deployed in the IP outsourcing industry.

"The importance of IP outsourcing is reinforced by the fact that many organisations lack the strategy and management expertise required to unlock the value of their IP asset. Moreover, it is not always cost efficient, strategically aligned or sometimes viable to build such expertise in-house."

4.1 The transactional model – an as-needed approach

This is the most widely used engagement model in which the organisation outsources the work to the service provider based on their internal requirements. This model is used by organisations where the requirements are sporadic, or the organisation already has an internal team to manage the work. This is a kind of pay-as-you-go service model.

Benefits of the transactional model: This model is relevant to those organisations which do not have a regular need for patent services. Therefore, for those organisations it neither makes business sense nor is it financially viable to recruit a full-time employee. For such firms, it is best to opt for a transactional model by engaging with an IP vendor who can cater to specific requirements. The primary benefit of this model is that there is no commitment and fixed cost associated with the service. An organisation can engage the service provider as and when needed. This model gives the organisation complete flexibility with no commitment or strings attached. The organisation can easily change the service provider if the existing service provider is unable to do the assigned work or is unable to help the organisation in achieving its underlying goals.

4.2 The FTE (full-time equivalent) model – a dedicated team approach

This is a model in which the service provider actually becomes an extended arm of the organisation. In this model, the service provider exclusively assigns and dedicates its resources for a specific period or for a long-term project. The FTE model allows the client to have complete control over the progress of the project. Dedicated resources are assigned to the project which the client can direct and monitor at will. An FTE resource is a dedicated, talented employee who works for the client.

Benefits of the FTE model: This model is more suited to those organisations which have a continuous and regular need for patent services. With this model, the organisation gets resources who dedicatedly work for them while eliminating the recruitment headaches and administrative hassles relating to employee management. The organisation employing this model focuses only on its core functions and the rest is taken care of by highly qualified candidates (without hiring one!) who work as an extended team. Moreover, the billing rates are much more economical compared with those in the transactional model or the hybrid model, described below. The FTE model is a transparent, secure, flexible and scalable way of working. The monthly cost is fixed which allows the organisation to manage its budget without the fear of price escalations.

4.3 The hybrid model

As the name suggests, this is a hybrid of the transactional and FTE models. It is a tailored model, which works best for firms which are in a transition phase, or are medium-sized firms, or are not particularly sure which of the two conventional models would work for them. With this model, the client does not engage a specific number of resources (as in the FTE model) and does not have a completely non-committal engagement (as in the transactional model). Instead, in the hybrid model, the client engages the service provider for either a minimum commitment of work or for a minimum commitment of cost over a fixed period. Since this model also requires an at least medium-term engagement, the client should have adequate confidence in the capability of the service provider before proceeding with this model.

Benefits of the hybrid model: This model is suitable for clients who do not have a continuous flow of work but require the assistance of the service provider at regular intervals. The minimum work commitment (either in terms of hours or cost) allows the client to have a deal that is financially better than that in the transactional model. Furthermore, the client does not incur any cost during the lean periods when no work is outsourced, as opposed to the FTE model where the costs continue.

5. Competencies of a good patent service provider

If you are considering outsourcing some or all of your core patent law functions to an external service provider, what are the characteristics that are most likely to produce a good experience for you and your clients? We believe that several stand out:

- A highly experienced IP team with the right skill set and patent domain expertise documented in their team profile.
- High levels of technical expertise, as documented in the team profile and individual profiles.
- The ability to perform in-depth analysis, as evidenced by sample reports and the service provider's explanation of how they execute their projects.
- A client-centric approach with customised services that demonstrate that they understand the objectives that you and your clients have for each project.
- Access to the leading commercial patent database(s) for the relevant industry sector, as documented by a list of the patent and non-patent databases that they use in their work.
- 'Star quality' demonstrated in sample reports that show a comprehensive, exhaustive approach and a serious quality review process.
- Fast turnaround, supported by reasonably firm assurances about the time required to execute the project.
- Cost-effectiveness, as evidenced by pricing that is reasonable for the complexity of the project but also competitive for the market.

Before commencing a project, you should require that the service provider review a statement of work (SoW) with you that includes, at a minimum:

- A brief overview of the client's objective.
- The methodology, with tentative timelines for interim progress as well as final deliverables.
- Payment terms.
- A sample analysis for a similar project.
- The deliverable format, so that you are aware what you are going to achieve, what the final output will look like, and when you will receive the final work product.

Always ask for an SoW from the service provider as this also gives you an opportunity to get the analysis or output or timelines tweaked and customised to your requirements before the project begins. Having the SoW in place at the start makes things easier for both parties and brings greater clarity to the discussion and the project.

6. Preparations and requirements before outsourcing

Once you are convinced that outsourcing is the best option for you and you have selected a patent service provider who suits your requirements and will be able to deliver the results that you seek, it is important to know more about the service provider and to verify certain aspects to ensure that your IP is in safe hands. The following list includes practices that will increase the likelihood that your needs and expectations will be met.

- Require the prospective service provider to provide, in a single form, the information that you will need to make a well-informed selection of your service provider. It should include basic company information, such as: the legal name of the company; the corporate structure of the company; its registered address and operating address; the number of employees; any litigation, arbitration, or other dispute resolution proceedings in which it is currently or has recently been involved as a party or witness; and, if the provider is located in a different jurisdiction from your own, any import/export licences it currently has.
- Execute the non-disclosure agreement and similar confidentiality agreements signed to ensure that your IP, confidential information and knowledge are absolutely safeguarded. This will create a confidential relationship between you and the service provider to protect any confidential and proprietary information or trade secrets.
- Ask the service provider for its written privacy policy document. This document will help you know how the service provider collects, handles and processes data of its customers and visitors. This document will explicitly describe whether that information is kept confidential or may be shared with or sold to third parties.
- Ask the service provider for its written conflict policy and conflict avoidance procedures, which will help you to understand how the provider handles various situations relating to conflict of interests among various parties.
- Be sure that you understand the service provider's approach towards data protection, that is, how they handle and process the personal information and data points.
- Ask the service provider about invoicing details (such as tax number (VAT/GST), company account number and other bank details). Having these details at the beginning serves two purposes: first, it gives you more confidence in the vendor; and second, once the project is successfully delivered, there will be no payment hassles.
- Finally, ask the vendor about their quality management system (QMS) and their quality control process (QCP). Find out whether the service provider's QCP includes client feedback. It is a good

pointer to check how much of the service provider's approach is client-centric. Generally, good service providers have 'client feedback' as a key part of the entire quality assurance process.

If a vendor has a robust QMS and QCP in place, it is highly unlikely that it would make any obvious errors in executing the project. A good QCP ensures that the project is thoroughly reviewed and a benchmark of the quality is maintained throughout the project. It is also important that the vendor delivers the project – 'right first time and every time' – without fail. This approach to quality injects creativeness into the overall process and supports ongoing process improvement. This is even more important for IP because the end result is subjective in nature; therefore, a robust QMS process, supported by clearly documented and functioning QCP standards, fosters quality consciousness in employees.

Once all the aforementioned requirements are met and a project SoW is submitted by the provider, the project can be more confidently assigned to the service provider. Also, make sure that during the course of the project you are getting regular updates from the provider. These updates could be interim deliverables, regular phone-calls, email exchanges and general updates, so that you are aware that

"It is important to have a healthy and transparent relationship with the IP service provider, both during the project and after it is done."

the project is on right path and there are no last-minute surprises. If you want, you may even decide a regular time interval for these updates at the commencement of the project. Once the project is delivered and meets your expectations, share your overall feedback with the service provider. After the project is delivered, within a couple of days, the service provider should raise the invoice. It is good practice to make the payment within the timeframe specified on the invoice. This will reassure the service provider and strengthen your relationship. It is important to have a healthy and transparent relationship with the IP service provider, both during the project and after it is done.

7. Conclusions

In this chapter, the various aspects and dimensions relating to outsourcing of patent drafting, research and analysis have been discussed. The chapter sheds light on the fact that outsourcing also provides a more effective operating environment at the backend, enabling a competitive edge over the potential competitors, aiming to enter the marketplace with a similar product, process or brand. Patent service providers can present an organisation with an optimal solution through efficient IP support functions, enabling the organisation to focus on its core business leading to increased productivity and

"If what counts is how an organisation uses its IP as a tool, then outsourcing this function to external IP vendors who are experts in identifying, developing, managing and leveraging IP makes commercial and strategic sense."

improved profitability. Further, for small and medium-size enterprises (SMEs) – such as most law firms – patents become far more important as they are light on other resources. To make sure that the SMEs leverage their patented technology, it is paramount for them to understand its value and engage a professional patent vendor who can take care of their IP assets and advise them on various fronts. Outsourcing of patent work by SMEs has now become economically viable and offers a number of advantages such as reduced costs, improved quality, domain expertise and quick turnaround time. Outsourcing enables the SMEs to concentrate their efforts and energies on their core competencies of product and service development and free themselves from the frequently time-consuming effort needed to manage, build and monetise their intangible assets. For SMEs in particular, outsourcing is more cost effective than recruiting a full-time employee, and cheaper still than hiring the strategy and administration skills required to deliver the service effectively. The patent service provider acts as an external expert and becomes the extended arm of the SME by providing various IP services and advice on all aspects relating to IP. Outsourcing the IP functions helps SMEs to reduce costs and thereby increase profitability.

Over the years, it has become increasingly clear that IP strategy and management is essential to an organisation as it drives performance, gives a competitive edge and helps an organisation to succeed. What matters is not the mere ownership of IP but how to unlock the true potential of the IP asset in possession. It is about creating the value out of the owned IP. If what counts is how an organisation uses its IP as a tool, then outsourcing this function to external IP vendors who are experts in identifying, developing, managing and leveraging IP makes commercial and strategic sense. Outsourcing is driven by the fundamental economic principle that specialisation increases economic efficiency. In an IP context, it allows the organisation to focus its resources on its area of expertise while having its IP assets managed by an IP external vendor that specialises in precisely this area.

Happy outsourcing!

8. Useful references

- World Intellectual Property Organization: www.wipo.int/.
- United States Patent and Trademark Office: www.uspto.gov/.
- European Patent Office: www.epo.org/.
- Intricate Research Pvt Ltd: www.intricateresearch.com/.
- IP Australia: www.ipaustralia.gov.au/patents.

Notes

1 Intricate Research is an IP research and analytics firm, based in India, with experience and expertise in providing patent and legal services worldwide at every stage of the patent life cycle, from drafting and prosecution to enforcement and litigation. With a blend of technical and legal knowledge, the firm provides patent research and analytics services. The firm's clientele includes IP law firms, patent licensing firms, patent brokers, legal departments at mid-sized companies, research institutions and universities.
2 CPC: Cooperative Patent Classification.
3 IPC: International Patent Classification.
4 USPC: United States Patent Classification.
5 FI: File Index (Japanese patent classification systems).
6 F-Term: File forming term (Japanese patent classification systems).

III. Outsourcing cybersecurity: the logical solution for legal practices

Sitima Fowler
Iconic IT[1]

1. Introduction

In the early days of computing, desktop machines were square, heavy and clunky. Keyboards made an annoyingly loud click-clacking sound and green, blinking cursors filled the small monitor screens. We used WordPerfect and floppy discs for storage, and we were thrilled with our dial-up internet. This is the same time that millions of people died virtually of dysentery in the classic PC game, *The Oregon Trail.* Through these early years, however, the first IT outsourcing services were already emerging, specialising in remote application management. Over the years, outsourced IT services have expanded and now include network repairs, backup and recovery solutions, cloud solutions, hardware upgrades and, of course, cybersecurity.

With cybersecurity comes cybercrime, and in 1981 the first 'serious' cyberattack occurred. That crime was as simple as hacking into a phone company's database and resetting its internal clock so its customers could have free long-distance calling during 'peak' hours. At the time, this was a genius act – and an omen of things to come.

Times have changed, and so has cybercrime. According to *Cybercrime Magazine*, cybercrime damages are predicted to reach $6 trillion globally by 2021. Law firms are fast-growing targets, with the American Bar Association's *2019 Legal Tech Report* concluding that

26% of law firms experienced a breach, and 36% had malware installed in their networks.[2] That doesn't sound like much until you break it down: approximately one in four law firms have experienced data breaches, and over one-third of all law firms have had malware disrupt their daily operations.

2. Why are smaller law firms targeted?

In the United States in 2016, a four-person law firm in Kansas was breached with a ransomware attack from an organised group called Dark Overlord. Data involving clients of an insurance company was compromised, and while the law firm did notify the FBI to investigate the breach, they ultimately ended up paying the ransom to have their data released. However, they failed to notify the insurance company they represented, or the insurance company's clients, that the breach occurred. Nearly two years later an employee from the insurance company stumbled across the news that the law firm, and subsequently the insurance company they represented, had been victims of a breach. The law firm ended up paying over $1.5 million in damages to the insurance company. The basis for the damages were that the law firm had negligently allowed the insurance company's information to be breached by not using proper security measures, and that the law firm had not made the proper notifications as required by federal and state regulatory agencies. In short, it was ruled that the law practice had not acted ethically in securing the proper protections for its client.[3]

Why are legal practices targeted by cybercriminals? Law firms may not realise that the very nature of what they do makes them appealing to hackers. The wealth of information kept by a law practice includes storing an enterprise's data, intellectual property and valuable data on corporate employees. Hackers only need to breach the firm to 'have it all'. It is far easier to hack one network and get information on all the practice's clients at once. Why rob the cash machine when they can rob the entire bank?

Law firms are a 'one stop shop' for both state actors and opportunistic hackers alike. It is a trifecta for cybercriminals: unlimited sensitive data on corporations and individuals alike, many clients, and very sensitive data make law firms an easy, profitable target for hackers.

Hackers can cause serious damage to clients which can include selling identities, financial fraud and more. Legal firms have an additional concern – the sensitive nature of their caseloads may include information bad actors can use to blackmail either the practice or the clients themselves.

The size of your law firm will not protect you; smaller law practices are

"The size of your law firm will not protect you; smaller law practices are targeted even more frequently than their larger counterparts. These practices may never recover from the breach and odds are not in their favour: an estimated 60% of all small businesses will shut their doors forever after just one incident."

targeted even more frequently than their larger counterparts. These practices may never recover from the breach and odds are not in their favour: an estimated 60% of all small businesses will shut their doors forever after just one incident.[4]

Cybercriminals target small to mid-sized law firms because they often tend to be lax about security solutions. In most cases, cybersecurity is not a priority for decision-makers. There is not enough money in the firm's budget, there is not enough time or expertise to implement comprehensive strategies, or they simply do not think they are at risk of an attack. Many small to medium-sized legal practices do not have the resources needed to protect their firms. Of those that do, 77% of internal IT leaders admit they do not have an effective cybersecurity plan in place to protect their employers.[5]

Your partners and associates work at the speed of 'now', upgrading technology without necessarily updating the security needed to protect it. Increased connectivity, more mobile devices and immediate remote access are all necessary for your practice to move quickly, but these also increase your network's vulnerabilities. For savvy cybercriminals, the combination of vulnerabilities and ineffective cybersecurity strategies is not just a welcome mat, it is a sign on the door reading *Try and Hack Me.*

Cybersecurity is a porch light you leave on at night. If your light is on, you significantly decrease the odds of a thief targeting your home. A would-be burglar will avoid your house and move on to the house next door that has no lights on, no barking dogs and no home security system. Likewise, hackers are drawn to law firms with ineffective security platforms and a lax attitude towards cybersecurity.

Cyberhackers have no end to the bag of tricks they use to discover vulnerabilities, including a vulnerability scanner. They find potential targets by surfing the internet, and when one is found, they infiltrate on the practice's front-facing services. From there, the hacker will launch bots to find other weaknesses on the network.

The best protection is prevention, securing all weaknesses and vulnerabilities so the hackers move on to the next target.

3. The trend: legal practices turn to MSPs or MSSPs for help
Many small to medium-sized law firms do not realise that outsourcing IT concerns such as cybersecurity, can reduce liability, save money, increase compliancy and improve their services. Your practice will not receive the cybersecurity solutions it needs to survive without a comprehensive IT approach. To meet this demand, law firms are increasingly turning to managed services providers (MSPs) and

"Cyberhackers have no end to the bag of tricks they use to discover vulnerabilities, including a vulnerability scanner."

managed security services providers (MSSPs) to outsource their cybersecurity needs.

Cybersecurity is an IT function that is too important to handle on your own, or even with a modest IT department. The implications of a single breach will cost you, both financially and reputationally. If your practice survives the initial breach, statistics show that it is likely to be targeted again.[6]

Professional cybersecurity experts know exactly how to react to a disaster. They understand how to limit damages and how to communicate with clients, employees and the press. An MSSP has the knowledge to get the law firm back up and running while avoiding the ransom, as well as how to submit a claim to the cyber risk insurance carrier for financial losses, business disruptions, penalties and other mitigation costs.

Outsourcing gives businesses the high-quality cybersecurity solutions they need to stay compliant with regulations, keep up to date on security trends and it will save them money.

There is no reasonable way a legal firm can keep ahead of financial regulatory guidelines; no matter where your practice is located you are responsible for knowing and following any number of laws and regulations relating to your country. For instance:

- OFAC (United States);
- General Data Protection Regulation (GDPR) (European Union);
- Financial Crimes Enforcement Network (FinCen) (United States);
- European Union;
- Her Majesty's Treasury (United Kingdom);
- French Ministry of Finance;
- Anti-money laundering (AML) laws;
- Office of the Comptroller of the Currency (OCC) (United States); and
- Financial Conduct Authority (United Kingdom).

Partnering with a cybersecurity specialist in your law firm's home country ensures your firm stays compliant with their unique financial requirements. Outsourcing cybersecurity services for legal practices is not just a good idea – the rising numbers of law firm security breaches show that it is crucial.

4. Outsourcing cybersecurity or in-house solutions?

Many smaller legal firms have an 'IT guy' or a small IT team, but outsourcing cybersecurity is still a good idea. As technology continues

"Some law firms are relying on a break-fix IT solution to try to save money. This means that problems are not addressed until they become big enough to cause a disruption in your daily operations."

to advance, cybersecurity specialists will offer updated and upgraded solutions that most internal IT departments are not able to, and often for far less money than is spent on the practice's current cybersecurity solutions.

Some law firms are relying on a break-fix IT solution to try to save money. This means that problems are not addressed until they become big enough to cause a disruption in your daily operations. By the time you call a professional to fix a problem, a small and manageable issue has become huge. These on-demand technical calls will end up costing law practices far more money than they would have spent had they been receiving proactive support with outsourced IT services. A 'rental technician' will not be familiar with your network and may spend as much time learning your infrastructure as on repairing the IT issues.

Using a break-fix model of managing your IT allows an incident to quickly spread throughout your entire network while you wait for your 'rental technicians' to identify the problem, pinpoint the affected devices and repair the damage the issue has caused.

Legal practices without an internal IT department may be trying to piece together their own cybersecurity platforms, relying on boxed 'solutions' (store and internet purchased 'one-size-fits-all' IT solutions) and pre-packaged cybersecurity software. The reality is that outsourced solutions are far more effective than boxed or free products and provide more complete coverage of cybersecurity gaps and vulnerabilities. Boxed solutions can cause compatibility issues with a legal firm's existing software and cause far more problems than they solve. A poorly configured security application can crash a network, delete important files, block safe applications and otherwise interfere with data and file storage and retrieval. Your most trusted legacy software may be incompatible with your chosen cybersecurity solutions, causing even more disruption.

It is easy to piece together boxed solutions or free software for cybersecurity, but these strategies are frequently faulty, incomplete and expensive. These 'solutions' do not go far enough in improving risk management and are usually more trouble than they are worth in both installation and implementation. A cybersecurity specialist has access to cutting-edge technology and strategies that law firms need to stay compliant, secure and within budget.

As bad actors evolve, cybersecurity platforms must also evolve. Anti-virus or email filtering software will quickly become outdated in this rapidly changing cybercrime landscape, making free solutions and boxed solutions an ineffective solution. These strategies may involve complicated user processes and be easily sidestepped by frustrated employees and may be difficult to install and update. In the end, the cost of sub-par products and the possibility of a breach despite installing these platforms makes boxed solutions a cost-prohibitive choice. Many of the current trends in outsourced cybersecurity, however, involve artificial intelligence (AI), automation and a system-friendly interface.

In today's cybersecurity world, a regular antivirus is not enough. Law practices need an AI-based antivirus that looks at each user's normal communication patterns and identifies, and blocks, any deviations. If a partner is in regular communication with an associate, for instance, AI will learn to identify that as normal communication for both. If the partner suddenly emails someone they are not normally in contact with, however, the AI process will take notice and scrutinise that email a little more to ensure it is from the partner and not a spear phishing attack.

Many law firms are using an AI-based antivirus; in fact, it is hard to find a current antivirus solution that does not employ basic AI. These programs by themselves, however, are no match for today's sophisticated hackers, because the criminals themselves use ever-evolving AI platforms to deploy their attacks. Only a cybersecurity specialist has access to the tools, combinations and complete cybersecurity platforms that law firms need to stay one step ahead of today's savvy cybercriminals.

Some more advanced MSSPs offer a security operations centre (SOC). A security operations centre is supported 24/7 by a team that continuously monitors the practice's network checking for alerts, inconsistencies and potential issues. This is a service far beyond what most internal IT departments can be expected to offer.

A firm's IT department may have too much on its plate. Tech burnout is real, and many IT techs report feeling overworked and pressured. These are the firefighters of the IT world; the focus is on putting out daily fires in your firm rather than proactively maintaining infrastructure or addressing cybersecurity concerns. The logical choice would be to hire more IT team members, but qualified IT techs are in great demand and therefore hard to find.

Outsourcing cybersecurity and a few other key IT functions keeps IT techs focused on daily operational IT needs. An MSP can take care of security issues such as backup and network testing, security patches, and proactively maintaining and monitoring the network while your existing IT department can keep on top of your practice's daily IT needs and projects.

Chances are that your IT department is still using the same anti-virus and spam-filtering software they have been using for years.

Figure 1. What is a security operations centre (SOC)?

A security operations centre is supported by security specialists who monitor and analyse the activity on your network, servers, endpoints, databases, applications, websites and other systems, looking for anomalous activity that could be indicative of a security incident. The SOC staff work closely with your IT support team to ensure that security issues are addressed quickly upon discovery.

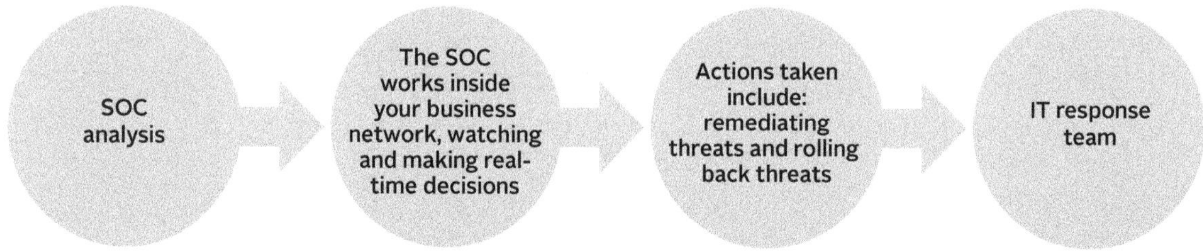

Unfortunately, the mindset of 'If it isn't broke, don't fix it' will not work when dealing with cybercrime. MSPs use automation and cutting-edge technology and tools that provide scalable solutions as the practice grows, changing the tech to meet evolving cybercrime. Remember, that while growth is good, growth also brings your practice to the attention of cybercriminals and your firm becomes an even more tempting target for hackers. Your internal IT department needs to stay one step ahead of cybercriminals, and this is a challenge they may be unable to meet on their own.

Because outsourcing cybersecurity does not mean completely replacing your IT staff, MSPs can work hand in hand with your existing IT department. Law practices can lighten the load on their IT teams by outsourcing time-consuming functions, such as cybersecurity.

Qualified MSPs give smaller legal practices the cybersecurity resources they need without hiring full-time personnel to staff an internal IT department or hiring additional staff to supplement an existing one. In addition, cybersecurity providers will have access to trends in technology that an internal IT department may not have, often at a lower price than the practice itself would pay for less effective cybersecurity solutions and tools.

It is the effectiveness of these tools and solutions that make outsourcing cybersecurity the best strategy for law firms. Using these tools, a cybersecurity specialist will spot vulnerabilities and weaknesses before the bad guys can act on them. An internal IT department will not have the resources needed to proactively monitor networks and stop cyber criminals in real-time, but an MSP will detect the malware before it can affect the network.

Unfortunately, when a breach occurs it is up to the law firm to prove that it took the necessary precautions to prevent it. Cyber risk insurance may not pay out on claims if appropriate steps were not taken to secure the network, and regulatory fines will be increased without proper proof of compliance.

If a law firm is relying on outdated technology, boxed solutions and an 'it won't happen to us' mindset, it is only a matter of time before a breach happens. There is no way to get comprehensive solutions with boxed products and free software, and ultimately your practice will pay the price in one way or the other.

5. Regulatory compliance is more complicated than ever before
In the United States, for example, there are few, if any, regulatory regimes that apply specifically to the collection, maintenance and security of information by law firms. However, general laws and

regulations applicable to all businesses sometimes have a special, and frequently overlooked, impact on law firms. For example, the American Bar Association has very specific guidelines on what should be considered moral and ethical behaviours for law firms. Moreover, in the United States, the Health Insurance Portability and Accountability Act (HIPAA)[7] has its reach into the legal world, regulating law firms that have access to any healthcare entities or patient information. A personal injury firm representing a client injured in an accident or an employee compensation case could have liability issues under the HIPAA if, for example, the client's health care records are called in evidence, or even just stored in a breached legal firm's database. Such a tiny oversight can cause huge problems for even the smallest of law firms.

In addition to federal regulations, lawyers in the United States are subject to numerous state regulatory agencies, with each state having its own unique requirements. Outside the United States, equally complex regulations can be found, such as the General Data Protection Regulation (GDPR)[8] in Europe and South Korea's Personal Information Protection Act (PIPA),[9] which is one of the strictest data protection regulations in the world. It is estimated that 66% of countries world-wide have data protection legislation in place,[10] with more coming on board as the cybercrime landscape continues to evolve.

Compliance issues have other consequences as well. Failure to maximise security efforts will make shopping for a cyber risk policy much harder. These providers will hit legal practices with higher premiums if they do not meet the provider's cybersecurity standards, which tend to be as stringent as regulatory requirements. In fact, an insurer is unlikely to cover a law firm that has thin, or non-existent, cybersecurity platforms. In-house cybersecurity solutions may give these companies the excuse they need to hold the legal practice accountable for security breaches and to justify its decision to avoid paying claims.

The penalties for violating privacy, unsafely sharing information and being lax regarding data storage can be punishable by stiff fines and fees, reputational loss, and in some extreme cases even a prison sentence. Even something as simple as updating your equipment and discarding old equipment without sanitising it properly (wiping all data from the device) will land you in the middle of regulatory complications. Law firms are realising that experienced cybersecurity providers can protect legal practices from these ever-changing rules and regulations. Law practices that have compliance programmes in place can sharply reduce their liability and fines even if a violation occurs. This alone makes outsourcing cybersecurity to an MSP a valuable cost-saving choice for any law firm.

6. What if your printer or security camera is a vulnerability?
The Internet of Things (IoT) is a newer buzzword that loosely covers any device connected to the internet. This includes automated systems such as thermostats, security cameras and printers. Each one of these 'things' is given a unique identifier and can automatically transfer data over a network.

Evolving connectivity means that just about anything with an on and off switch can be attached to your network and set to alert, start, turn off, adjust, print, scan, or any other action you can imagine. While the idea of your office's thermostat turning off at night and back on in the morning sounds harmless, remember that every device connected to your network is a potential vulnerability.

In the United States in 2016, the small and unremarkable Bowman Dam in Rye, New York, became the unlikely target of a state-sponsored cyberattack. The bad actors accessed the dam's automated computer processes which were continuously updated by sensors in the water. These computer guided sensors relayed water levels and temperatures back to the main computer program. The flow rates in the dam then automatically adjusted based on the information communicated by these sensors.

"Many boxed cybersecurity solutions are not sophisticated enough to protect all connected devices, leaving vulnerabilities in your practice that savvy cybercriminals can breach."

The computer program was accessible through a cellular modem, and it was this weakness that was exploited by the hackers. With this access in place, the cybercriminals could have easily opened the gates and flooded the small city. The bad actors did not use the information for damage, but it seemed to be a warning. For cybersecurity professionals, this incident was an eye-opener into the vulnerabilities that can be caused when the IoT is breached.[11]

IoT hacks are very subtle and less likely to be noticed, but these devices give the hackers all the access they need to breach your network. Many boxed cybersecurity solutions are not sophisticated enough to protect all connected devices, leaving vulnerabilities in your practice that savvy cybercriminals can breach.

7. Trending cyberthreats for law firms

Ransomware remains one of the primary malware attacks that bad actors use to breach legal practices. This mode of attack is usually deployed accidentally by a user. Ransomware is a tricky malware to remove, leaving legal practices torn between paying the ransom and hoping the bad actors will return their files, or trying to restore the data on their own. The costs of the ransom are painful enough, but the cost of waiting for data to be restored can hurt even more.

In May 2020, it was reported that targeted cyberattacks were rapidly becoming a security nightmare for many law firms of all sizes. In the span of five months, seven legal practices were victims of ransomware. All these attacks were carried out by two highly organised cybercriminal groups, one known as REvil and the other calling itself Maze.[12]

Maze was responsible for holding the data of five law firms 'hostage' during this time. The organisation released HIPAA consent forms, personal injury case pain diaries, and other sensitive data of one unlucky practice. The activities of Maze were particularly alarming because, rather than just threatening to release data, the group published bits of data to prove their threat was real.

REvil was another organisation at work during this time. This group was responsible for hacking into a large law firm that represented many high-profile celebrities as well as breaching an 11-attorney law firm, proving that the size of the practice did not matter. In both hacks, sensitive data was released.

Cybercriminals are no longer found only in dark, smoke-filled basements, working alone. Cybercrime has evolved to be big business and is as organised as any business can be. From terrorist organisations to lone-wolf hackers, your law firm is at risk.

"Cybercriminals are no longer found only in dark, smoke-filled basements, working alone. Cybercrime has evolved to be big business and is as organised as any business can be."

Hacktivists, for instance, are cybercriminals with an agenda, usually targeting an organisation because of its beliefs, political ties or affiliations. The end goal of hacktivists is usually to disrupt and cripple an organisation. If your law firm is representing well-known clients with political ties, for example, your practice may be at risk for hacktivists to launch an attack.

On the other hand, insider threats originate a little closer to home. These are disgruntled or negligent employees, or even individuals from rival law practices 'planted' in your firm. Insider threats cover a wide range of attack modes, from attackers deliberately launching malware to employees accidentally clicking infected files or links. According to a 2018 Ponemon study,[13] insider threats are on the rise. One example of an insider threat occurred when a Texas-based law firm in the United States was hacked by a former IT engineer who had worked for the firm for five years. The engineer had the knowledge to access the firm's database without authorisation causing, according to the US Attorney's office of the Northern District of Texas, "significant damage to the network".[14]

Organised cybercriminal groups specialise in advanced persistent threats (APTs) and are usually (but not always) state sponsored. These groups attack to mine for information or disrupt organisations, with many organised groups striking for money for their own countries or to uncover military and political secrets from rival countries. With nearly infinite funding and the combined knowledge of many different 'hacking professionals' under the same virtual roof, these groups are especially dangerous.

Lone-wolf cybercriminals act alone, usually looking for financial reward. The information this hacker gains will be sold on the dark web or used to steal money directly from your law firm or your clients. Lone-wolf hackers include internet stalkers who may target a firm's managing partners or associates, or the rogue state-sponsored actor who is working alone rather than as part of a larger, organised group.

Phishing scammers focus on email scams, such as infected links, spoofed websites and 'urgent' information requests. These bad actors do not necessarily target one specific law firm; they attack many practices at once in the hope that someone, from any firm, will interact with them. It is a 'throw something at the wall and see what sticks' approach rather than a focused one.

Your legal practice is vulnerable to attacks from any of these bad actors and, depending on the nature of your firm's services, possibly more than one of them. As if this was not alarming enough, there is a frightening trend on the dark web which could also affect your practice.

Imagine a world where cybercriminals can go online and order cyberattack software as easily as ordering a shirt from a website. Thanks to the dark web, this happens every day.

There is an entire industry focused on supplying cybercriminals with the tools they need to build their own malware. Called Malware as a Service (MaaS) or sometimes Cybercrime as a Service (CaaS), this software and hardware is leased to individuals for the sole purpose of carrying out cyberattacks. As unbelievable as it sounds, MaaS websites offer full services – a botnet to distribute the malware, a personal account used to launch the attack, and even technical support come with these malware packages. MaaS suppliers organise their services like a typical business model, working nine to five when employees are most typically at their desks and networks are most vulnerable.

One example of MaaS was 2017's ransomware exploit, GandCrab. GandCrab's malware was designed to be both easily deployed by hackers and easily resolved by the victims of the business targeted. GandCrab made it easier for targets to pay the ransom than it was to remove the malware, hoping that victims would rather pay a smaller ransom than take the time to find and remove the threat. The creators of GandCrab found that many companies were willing to pay the ransom to release data rather than face downtime, lost productivity and the cost of hiring a technician to remove the malware.

GandCrab could be found on hacking forums. In return for providing the malware, the developers of GandCrab kept 60% of the ransom fees collected by its users. GandCrab gave its customers the malware, then backed it up with updates, incident tracking systems and ongoing support.[15]

Cybercriminals using products provided by MaaS can focus on a single entity or many organisations at the same time. Since a business falls victim to a cyberattack every 13 seconds (according to a *Cyber Defense Magazine* report),[16] hackers can play the numbers game and know that one of their attacks will be successful. With automation behind them, a cyberattack that fails the first time can be continuously deployed until it succeeds. Because modern malware is becoming increasingly subtle, it can take organisations up to six months or more to realise they have been breached.[17]

The purchasers of the packaged MaaS malware do not even have to be tech-savvy to launch a devastating attack. The programs are designed to be user friendly and can target everything in a network from the servers to the machines, and even devices connected through the IoT.

8. Outsourced cybersecurity services provided by an MSP
The best cybersecurity solutions are supported by technicians giving oversight to all aspects of the strategies offered. Internal IT departments usually do not have the resources to support a comprehensive cybersecurity strategy, but an MSP has the flexibility, resources, personnel, knowledge and high-tech tools required to maintain an effective security plan.

The cybersecurity solutions offered by an MSP frequently involve layers of strategies and solutions rather than one stand-alone product. These solutions usually involve a mix of effective cybersecurity strategies to protect networks, email clients, devices, applications and files.

Outsourced cybersecurity solutions include a powerful combination of firewall defences, anti-malware and anti-virus products, anti-spam and email filtering software, cloud storage solutions, comprehensive backup, recovery and business continuity plans, cybersecurity awareness training for employees, event log monitoring, testing and phishing simulations to assess network and user preparedness, dark web scans and monitoring, routine re-assessments of strategies, updated security patches, and other scalable solutions.

"With an estimated 91% of successful cyberattacks infecting the network through phishing, business email compromise, spoofing and other email strikes, protections such as spam filtering and blocking are an important part of any cybersecurity strategy."

To keep on top of a firm's needs, many MSPs are redefining and adding roles. One of these positions is a Technical Alignment Coordinator (TAC). The role of the TAC is to perform an initial audit and create an IT roadmap for the practice, then perform an ongoing assessment with routine on-site visits. The TAC's visits are to look for gaps and changes that will affect the firm's roadmap, including re-prioritising the IT budget, looking for data changes, checking for regulatory compliance updates, personnel changes, and other things that may affect the initial plan. Because most small firms are working with limited budgets, the TAC's responsibilities will involve finding ways to save the practice money.

The services and products received in a cybersecurity package will vary among MSPs, but there are a few key strategies which are universal.

With an estimated 91% of successful cyberattacks infecting the network through phishing, business email compromise, spoofing and other email strikes, protections such as spam filtering and blocking are an important part of any cybersecurity strategy. Email protection is only a part of the plan, however, and is only as effective as the person using it. Cybersecurity awareness training will be provided to ensure that all employees in the practice can recognise email attacks and avoid clicking infected links, supplying sensitive data to suspicious sources, or downloading malicious files. Part of this training will include simulated phishing attacks to gauge an employee's readiness to spot false emails and provide additional training if necessary.

Another part of a successful cybersecurity plan is general network protections. These will involve tools such as firewalls, anti-malware and antivirus software. The MSP will continuously monitor the practice's network for suspicious activity, outdated software and security patches that need to be installed. The cybersecurity network protections offered by a cybersecurity expert will also include DNS filtering that blocks suspicious or malicious websites, and makes sure inappropriate content is blocked. Routine scans will ensure that none of the firm's data has been released on the dark web.

Backup and recovery solutions are an important part of any outsourced cybersecurity strategy, along with a business continuity plan to reduce downtime and quickly restore data in case of a natural disaster, breach or even user error. These solutions frequently involve cloud services.

9. Moving your network to the cloud

Cloud services are not only an important part of cybersecurity, but they also save legal firms money in equipment by passing the purchase, maintenance and other hardware costs back to the cloud provider. Cloud services improve connectivity and communication, allowing associates to have any of the firm's notes or files at their fingertips, wherever they are.

While cloud services provide improved mobility and connectivity, they also allow more devices to access the firm's network. Every device connected remotely is an additional security concern. MSPs offer endpoint protections that cover all the devices connected to the network, even remotely, and will include strategies such as multi-factor logins, password protections and data encryption.

The US National Security Agency has grouped cloud vulnerabilities into the following four main classifications.[18]

- **Misconfiguration:** This vulnerability frequently arises from mistakes and misunderstandings of shared responsibility. This is a vulnerability that can be mitigated through better employee training with a focus on helping employees understand the concept of cloud security and its potential weaknesses.
- **Poor access controls:** When good access practices are not followed, such as multi-factor authentication and rigorous

"One of the first financial benefits to outsourcing cybersecurity is clarity. It allows legal firms to implement resource planning, a valuable tool for practices to help define IT costs and create a solid cybersecurity budget."

password requirements, a vulnerability arises where security measures can be by-passed by hackers. When there are poor access controls in place for cloud computing, sensitive information is not properly protected.
- **Shared tenancy:** Shared tenancy vulnerabilities occur when a hacker can unravel the combination of hardware and software solutions a law firm uses to gain access to cloud data. This is best countered with encryption and a trusted cloud services provider.
- **Supply chain vulnerabilities:** Supply chain vulnerabilities usually begin at the level of the cloud provider and involve intentional weaknesses, such as backdoor applications, that are inserted within the hardware or software used to access the cloud. Again, using a trusted cloud services provider is the best way to mitigate supply chain vulnerabilities.

Professional IT services providers use trusted cloud services providers, and they have solutions to detect and block these vulnerabilities before they take a foothold in your network.

Cloud services are frequently offered in an outsourced cybersecurity strategy as part of the practice's business continuity plan. When the firm's files are protected in the cloud, backup and recovery can happen rapidly rather than taking days or even weeks to restore deleted or corrupted data.

It is more than just sending data to the cloud, however; backup solutions must be routinely tested to ensure they are ready to deploy when needed. An MSP will be able to do this for legal practices without disrupting daily operations.

Cloud services are available to law firms without outsourcing their cybersecurity, but these stand-alone cloud solutions are less secure, unreliable and more costly than those offered by an MSP. An MSP will have a special relationship with cloud services providers, meaning they can negotiate services and protections for a lower price than the practice's IT department could on its own.

10. Outsourcing cybersecurity and cost savings

Small to medium-sized legal practices will find that outsourcing cybersecurity will save them money in many ways, from proactive solutions to fight cybercrime to money saved on cyber risk insurance and decreased regulatory violations.

One of the first financial benefits to outsourcing cybersecurity is clarity. It allows legal firms to implement resource planning, a valuable tool for practices to help define IT costs and create a solid cybersecurity budget. Purchasing cybersecurity services provides a dependable roadmap that allows the firm to understand what they are receiving, how much they will be paying and how long it will take to deploy the solutions. Your MSP will provide a scalable plan, and the cybersecurity strategies will align with your firm's goals and grow with your practice.

Another cost-saving feature of outsourced cybersecurity is its ability to extend the reach of your internal IT department. An MSP will provide tools and resources that make the IT department's job easier. The IT department is free to focus on daily operational IT concerns while the MSP or MSSP can focus on larger projects and cybersecurity strategies.

Your cybersecurity services will save you money by ensuring your security platforms are always running efficiently, your spam and email filters are updated, security patches are installed, all equipment is protected and upgraded, and all software is brought up to date. These important cybersecurity protections cover the vulnerabilities that hackers look for when planning an attack, although these strategies may fall through the cracks of an overworked IT department.

With most MSPs moving security to the cloud, outsourced cybersecurity will decrease downtime after an incident. Retrieving and restoring data from the cloud takes minutes or hours rather than days. This ease of remediation following a disruptive incident gets you back in touch with your clients much faster than your internal IT department or manual solutions can.

Other security precautions will be included in your cybersecurity plan, such as end-to-end encryption, multifactor authentication, password protections and cybersecurity awareness training for all partners, associates and other employees in your practice. Because MSPs have partnerships with third-party providers, they can purchase these products and services for less money than your IT department can.

Limited budgets make the expansion of your IT department cost prohibitive. Not only are qualified IT technicians hard to find, but they also command a premium salary. In addition to hiring these techs, your law firm will need to provide ongoing training for them as well as their workstations and equipment. Partnering with an MSP means having on-demand IT personnel available without the added expense of adding them to the payroll.

11. Finding the right cybersecurity outsourcing services

There is a saying, 'If it walks like a duck and quacks like a duck, it's a duck'. That is not entirely true when you are considering outsourcing your cybersecurity concerns.

"Your cybersecurity services will save you money by ensuring your security platforms are always running efficiently, your spam and email filters are updated, security patches are installed, all equipment is protected and upgraded, and all software is brought up to date."

Many MSPs claim to have expertise in law firm needs, but a closer look at their service plans reveals the opposite. When you are looking for a reputable MSP, never assume that what you see on the surface is what you will get. Look for cybersecurity services that provide, at a minimum:

- **Information security analysts:** This team is responsible for monitoring and maintaining your law practice's security and integrity of your data. They do this by conducting vulnerability testing and ongoing risk analysis, performing external and internal security audits, vetting third-party vendors to ensure compliancy and security, updating your disaster recovery, scaling your firm's incident response and business continuity plans, and other security metrics.
- **Technology alignment coordinator (TAC):** This role is critical to the ongoing maintenance of cybersecurity. The TAC performs an initial audit and creates an IT roadmap for the practice, then performs ongoing assessments with routine on-site visits.
- **Routine upgrades and timely security patches:** Cybercrime is not static, and your cybersecurity plans should not be either. Hackers can take advantage of the window of opportunity between finding a vulnerability and when it is addressed, a process known as a 'zero-day exploit'.[19] The more time that

lapses before a vulnerability is fixed, the more damage can be done to your network. Timely installation of security patches and updates, as well as routine maintenance, will protect your practice from these opportunistic attacks.

- **Backup and recovery plans:** Backup and recovery plans are more than just a cybersecurity concern. They mitigate any incident that interferes with your data storage, including natural disasters, accidental data deletion and power outages. An MSP should provide you with a comprehensive plan that includes a business continuity plan and a plan for rapid restoration of deleted or corrupted data.
- **Transparent pricing:** Surprises can be fun, but not when it involves your budget. Make sure you understand the inclusions and limits of your plan before you sign on the dotted line.
- **Compliance:** Your legal practice has unique regulations, rules, recommendations and laws. It is important that your cybersecurity outsourcing service is compliant with your local and national regulations. This means that both the MSP and any outside third-party vendors dealing with them are compliant as well.
- **Proactive approach:** A reputable MSP will provide a proactive approach, including notifying you of any vulnerabilities or incidents involving your firm's network. Maintenance and monitoring are an important part of proactively protecting your network.
- **Advanced cybersecurity protections:** In a world of sophisticated cybercriminals, even MSPs are not immune from breaches. Just as hackers target law firms for the most data they can find in one place, an MSP is a goldmine for cybercriminals. Some MSPs outsource their own cybersecurity to add an extra layer of protection for their clients. Make sure the MSP has its own data protected.
- **Local offices:** Your MSP should be located near to your practice for in-person responses and service. Having a local MSP makes it far easier to build a relationship and establish trust with your technicians and engineers and allows representatives to come to your office in person for cybersecurity testing and analysis. While most smaller-scale IT issues can be handled remotely, larger ones may require a technician to come to your offices and a visit by a local technician would be much quicker and easier to arrange.

You need to be sure the outsourcing service will be a good match for your practice. Ask pointed questions, such as:

- How familiar are you with the legal industry's compliance regulations?
- Will you provide training to our employees?
- How do you protect your own data?
- How long will your cybersecurity plans take to deploy?
- Who reviews and updates your processes?
- What do you believe is the biggest threat to the legal industry in general, and specifically to our practice?
- What will you need from our firm to create your strategy?
- How will you communicate with our firm, and who is our main point of contact here?

When looking for the right MSP or MSSP, do not be afraid to check references or testimonials from their existing clients. It is also a good idea to talk to your peers and find out who they are currently using or who they recommend.

12. Your responsibility after outsourcing your cybersecurity
Once your cybersecurity has been outsourced, you can't just 'set it and forget it'. Make sure you fully understand the risks to your practice, even with a cybersecurity strategy in place. You will need to provide oversight to the outsourcing partner to make sure all requirements are being met and no shortcuts are taken.

Compliance is important, for instance, but if cybersecurity standards are set just high enough for your law firm to pass regulatory audits, you are playing a risky game. Remember that compliance-based cybersecurity rules are the minimum a legal practice needs to avoid violations, and not necessarily the best solutions for your firm. It is important to understand the cybersecurity strategies your MSP is outlining for you, and make sure the solutions cover your firm completely.

Remember to expect the unexpected. Even the best cybersecurity strategy may fall flat if an employee clicks a malicious file. Encourage your MSP to test your firm's readiness for a security incident, and make sure your mitigation and remediation playbook is updated as strategies and solutions change. Your playbook should include notifications, backup strategies and statement of purpose (SOP) for all members of your team. Resiliency in the face of a cyber incident will rely on the responses of your team during an emergency. Your MSP will be able to get your firm back to business as usual if your own team is responsive, organised and aware of their roles in an emergency.

Make sure your team knows how to react if their devices are infected. From isolating the device by powering down and unplugging it to notifications, your employees should understand the steps they should take when faced with an incident.

Outsourcing cybersecurity will give you better cyber risk insurance rates but check your policy to ensure you maintain enough insurance to cover your potential losses, including income, reputational rebuilding, legal fees and violations. Work with your cybersecurity team to assess how much insurance you would need to protect your firm, recover financially and save your reputation following a breach.

Unless you are outsourcing all your IT, your internal IT department will still be responsible for daily operational IT needs. It is vital that you and your MSP are aligned regarding roles and responsibilities regarding your cybersecurity and your general IT concerns. Outsourcing vendors will take on the responsibility of cybersecurity, but it is up to your firm to keep them apprised of important updates, like hiring new third-party vendors, reporting lost or stolen equipment, and personnel changes.

13. Bringing it all together

With the average cost of a law firm breach topping US$7 million,[20] most small to mid-sized practices would not survive even a single incident. These estimated costs cover liabilities such as malpractice lawsuits, repairing the network, hiring forensic investigators to trace the hack, regulatory violations and business disruption. Reputational damage control can be costly and, for many law firms, completely ineffective due to the sensitive and privileged information the practice routinely handles. You are at risk of clients leaving your practice, even those not affected by the breach itself.

Cyber risk insurance is helpful – to a point. According to a 2019 article published by *CPO Magazine* in 2017, the loss ratio on cyber risk policies was 32%.[21] Break it down a little more, and that means for every US$1 million businesses spent on insurance premiums, the pay-out was only US$320,000.

Cybersecurity continues to evolve beyond the point where any boxed solutions can keep up, and many internal IT departments are not able to implement successful strategies to protect the network. Also, your internal IT department may be 'stagnant', meaning it is only accustomed to working with your firm and is not aware of trending cybersecurity threats. Your firm will benefit from the tools, expertise and resources of an expanded IT team without the costs of hiring more personnel.

Outsourcing cybersecurity removes much of the liability from your

"Outsourcing cybersecurity removes much of the liability from your firm if an incident occurs and will decrease any fines or legal action taken by regulatory agencies."

firm if an incident occurs and will decrease any fines or legal action taken by regulatory agencies. In addition, having an MSP or MSSP create and implement your cybersecurity plan will help your firm qualify for a better policy with lower premiums, and ensure your cyber risk insurance carrier will pay claims arising from an incident.

By partnering with an outsourced cybersecurity provider, your legal firm will benefit from reduced pricing on products and services, an affordable and complete cybersecurity plan, and cost savings resulting from proactive maintenance and monitoring.

With law firms increasingly becoming the targets for cybercrime, it is not a matter of if your firm will be breached, but when. Most smaller law firms do not have the benefit of large IT budgets and nearly infinite finances that larger firms do; if a small firm is breached, it usually means the end of the practice.

For larger legal firms, a dedicated internal IT department may be a logical solution. However, for small to medium-sized legal practices, outsourcing cybersecurity is more than just a cost-effective solution; it just makes sense.

Notes

1 Iconic IT is a provider of external technology and cybersecurity management services, based in the United States, with a specialised practice in law firms.
2 American Bar Association, "2019 Cybersecurity" (16 October 2019), www.americanbar.org/groups/law_practice/publications/techreport/abatechreport2019/cybersecurity2019/.
3 Mark Rasch, "Insurance Client Sues Small Law Firm $1.5M for Dark Overlord Payment", *Security Boulevard* (20 April 2020), https://securityboulevard.com/2020/04/insurance-client-sues-small-law-firm-1-5m-for-dark-overlord-payment/.
4 Council of Insurance Agents and Brokers, "Majority of Small Companies Lose Business After Undergoing Cyber-Attacks", *Leader's Edge* (undated), www.ciab.com/resources/majority-small-companies-lose-business-undergoing-cyber-attacks/.
5 Conner Forrest, "Report: 77% of Companies Don't Have a Consistent Cybersecurity Response Plan", *Tech Republic* (14 March 2018), www.techrepublic.com/article/report-77-of-companies-dont-have-a-consistent-cybersecurity-response-plan/.
6 Luis A Aguilar, "The Need for Greater Focus on the Cybersecurity Challenges Facing Small and Midsize Businesses", US Securities Exchange Commission (19 October 2015), www.sec.gov/news/statement/cybersecurity-challenges-for-small-midsize-businesses.html.
7 Pub.L. 104-191, 110 Stat. 1936 (1996).
8 Journal L119, 4 May 2016, pp1–88.
9 See Personal Information Protection Commission (Government of the Republic of Korea), "Personal Data Protection Laws", www.privacy.go.kr/eng/laws_policies_list.do.
10 Compliancy Group, "Law Firm HIPAA Compliance" (28 February 2020), https://compliancy-group.com/law-firm-hipaa-compliance/. See also, United Nations Conference on Trade and Development, "Data Protection and Privacy Legislation Worldwide" (2019), https://unctad.org/en/Pages/DTL/STI_and_ICTs/ICT4D-Legislation/eCom-Data-Protection-Laws.aspx, which presents an interactive world map of national data protection and privacy legislation.
11 Mark Thompson, "Iranian Cyber Attack on New York Dam Shows Future of War", *Time* (24 March 2016), https://time.com/4270728/iran-cyber-attack-dam-fbi/.
12 Victoria Hudgins, "Meet the Hacker Groups Snatching Law Firms' Client Data", *Law.com* (21 May 2020), www.law.com/legaltechnews/2020/05/21/meet-the-hacker-groups-snatching-law-firms-client-data/.
13 Larry Ponemon, "Data Breaches Caused by Insiders Increase in Frequency and Cost", Ponemon Institute (26 April 2018), www.ponemon.org/news-updates/blog/security/data-breaches-caused-by-insiders-increase-in-frequency-and-cost.html.
14 John G Browning, "Why Cybercriminals Are Targeting Law Firms", *D CEO* (July–August 2016), www.dmagazine.com/publications/d-ceo/2016/july-august/cybercrime-targets-law-firms/.
15 Brian Laing, "Malware-as-a-Service: The 9-to-5 of Organized Cybercrime", *Lastline* (8 March 2018), www.lastline.com/blog/malware-as-a-service-the-9-to-5-of-organized-cybercrime/.
16 InfoSec Newsflash, "Cyber Security Statistics for 2019", *Cyber Defense Magazine* (21 March 2019), www.cyberdefensemagazine.com/cyber-security-statistics-for-2019/.
17 Devon Mikovich, "15 Alarming Cyber Security Facts and Stats", *Cybint* (20 June 2020), www.cybintsolutions.com/cyber-security-facts-stats/.
18 National Security Agency, "Mitigating Cloud Vulnerabilities" (21 January 2020), https://media.defense.gov/2020/Jan/22/2002237484/-1/-1/0/CSI-MITIGATING-CLOUD-VULNERABILITIES_20200121.PDF.
19 Dirk AD Smith, "5 Examples of Zero-Day Attacks", *Networkworld* (12 August 2013), www.networkworld.com/article/2168888/5-examples-of-zero-day-attacks.html.
20 Wolters Kluwer, "Law Firm Cybersecurity" (2016), https://ct.wolterskluwer.com/sites/default/files/Law_Firm_Cybersecurity.pdf.
21 Nicole Lindsey, "Businesses Are Finding Out That Cyber Insurance Coverage Might Not Be What They Thought", *CPO Magazine* (31 January 2019), www.cpomagazine.com/cyber-security/businesses-are-finding-out-that-cyber-insurance-coverage-might-not-be-what-they-thought.

IV. Case studies in the evolution, issues and opportunities of document review

Karl Schieneman
Baia do Joao Eco Pousada

1. The perspective of a personal journey
Why does a pousada owner in a resort area in Brazil decide to look into his past professional life and write a best-practices narrative on document review?

This chapter presents a unique perspective of the author's professional and business history, from the beginning of large-scale document review in the United States in the 1990s to the current leveraging of technology to support innovations such as the use of remote reviewers working from home. The COVID-19 pandemic makes this chapter especially important because remote review, if adopted by more organisations, could keep document reviewers safer than working near other reviewers in an office building or review centre.[1] My goal is to help prospective customers of outsourced document review services to understand better and in more detail the operational issues inherent in the document review process, especially as it has been enhanced by technology, so that a decision to outsource this large, time-consuming and high-risk function will be better-informed and more likely to be successful for law firms, in-house corporate law departments and their clients.[2]

My history in document review starts in 1993, when, as a law firm associate, I spent over two years and 4,000 hours doing document review in a major securities case. This was at the beginning of the use of document management systems, which at the time no one really knew how to use, but which we needed, given the volume of documents involved. Then, in 1998–2004 and 2012–2020, I created and sold two of the fastest-growing review companies in the United States. In the first company, we staffed large litigations, investigations and complex transactions requiring up to 240 attorneys at a time, which in 2003 were the largest document reviews in the United States. In 2008, I changed my focus to technology to learn some new skills and helped to develop technology-assisted review templates and models, culminating in the staffing of the first contested review in the country to use artificial intelligence.[3]

I then decided to revisit document review seeking to capitalise on technology assisted review. I developed the first testing model and predictive software to identify the best attorneys for document review projects in the United States, which increased the speed and accuracy of picking review attorneys based solely on performance instead of availability and geography. I used this software as the first court-appointed Special Master for electronic discovery in the $1.2 billion Garlock bankruptcy case[4] and picked a remote review team to redact 1.2 million documents using artificial intelligence. These 11 review attorneys finished a very high-profile review in six weeks, while saving almost $1 million in review costs.

Based on these results, I convinced some large law firms to experiment with remote document review models, using review attorneys spread across the United States, instead of at a 'bricks and mortar' review centre.[5]

My exploratory work in the Brazilian legal market identified the impact that better document review could have on much of the world outside of the United States. This dispelled the myth that countries which have a disclosure-based litigation model, rather than the US discovery-based model, would not benefit from better document review practices. For this reason, jurisdictions with less experience in document review should find my 'lessons learned' to be useful, regardless of whether the review functions are performed on-site or remotely.

The technology section of this chapter offers a view into exploring document review with new technology and shares some perspectives on the challenges of merging review with technology and the opportunities of taking these risks. The last sections focus on developing the remote review model and tools to improve responses to some of the practical issues with on-site reviews. They also describe the challenges that remote, technology-assisted document review faced and the practical hurdles I had to cross to gain acceptance. Lastly, I will describe some open issues and opportunities for further development in the future.

2. Do differences in litigation rules among countries make document review unnecessary in most jurisdictions?

2.1 Discovery and privilege in the United States

The United States does the most document review projects and has an active industry of review attorneys looking for jobs. As part of this development, parties in US litigation negotiate how to produce electronic records in a process called *discovery*. In cases in the federal litigation system in the United States, parties have a right to ask the other party for the types of data they want, as well as the types of searches to be done to find documents to be used in the case. Because so much data is stored on devices, it would be impossible to review all potential data in a case. So parties use filters like key words or date ranges to reduce the scope of data that must be produced to the other side. Parties will often agree on a list of key words to run searches for data to be reviewed for relevancy by an attorney before it is produced. Lawyers can also help clients by sharing and talking about documents without having their assistance being disclosed. This concept is called *privilege.*

"Protecting privileged documents and communications from being revealed is another unique aspect of the discovery system."

Protecting privileged documents and communications from being revealed is another unique aspect of the discovery system. Once a privileged communication is found, potentially the entire collection of privileged documents may be open to discovery as well. As a result, documents which have a lawyer's involvement must be scrutinised during the review to prevent a violation of privilege and their production to the other side. This adversarial process results in a substantial amount of cost arising from reviewing the records before a court comes close to rendering an opinion.

2.2 The 'disclosure standard' in most of the rest of the world

Most of the world disagrees with this model and uses some type of 'disclosure standard'. In that process, the parties select their own data to produce based on data which supports their positions. Parties can disclose as much or as little information as they want to the other side. Between the two approaches, it is easy to see how the disclosure standard can reduce and control the amount of review done. By contrast, in the United States the adversary has the opportunity to ask for data which causes review costs to be much higher.

So does the document-review process, which originated in the United States, apply to legal systems and litigation in the rest of the world?[6] There are two responses:

- First, it is the growth of data which is creating more review and not the type of rules – discovery or disclosure – that a jurisdiction follows. Even if you and your client control how much you review, finding evidence to help your case is very difficult when our smart devices and 24/7 communications make it ever harder to find the useful data buried by other data. Electronic evidence is usually the best and most persuasive evidence. Humans lie or forget the truth. Having electronic records that support a litigation position strengthens the case put in front of judges or juries.
- Secondly, and more importantly, government investigations around the world tend to play out exactly like US discovery rules. Government investigators in countries that follow disclosure rules want to find the evidence, and they follow an approach similar to discovery by asking parties to reveal the types of documents that they want produced for analysis for potential regulatory violations. These investigations can turn into large review projects in any country.

The Volkswagen emissions fraud investigations in Germany demonstrated how government investigations outside the United States became a catalyst for changing how review is done internationally.[7] That review lasted over a year. Document reviewers learned on the fly how to capture and preserve data and then to review it to identify what they had to produce. The investigations around the world forced them to accept discovery concepts from regulators asking for tremendous amounts of data. These documents worked their way into the civil litigation that followed the regulatory investigations.

Brazil has had a similar experience. One of the biggest document reviews in Brazil covered South America and brought down a presidency. Operation Car Wash investigated payments to executives at the Brazilian-owned energy company, Petrobras, from construction contractors in order to be selected for large oil projects. The investigation had over 1,000 search warrants, expanded to 11 countries, and implicated politicians and a large construction company called Odebrecht.

Some Brazilian lawyers with whom I spoke described how they handled the investigation and their reactions to the output of the document production and reviews. After initially saying that the disclosure rules system used in Brazil made document review less critical, the quality of the large document reviews, such as Operation Car Wash, was an issue. They agreed that there were gaps in the records received and that documents they would have expected to have received were missing. The Brazilian law firms that were involved, in most cases, were not large by US or UK standards, and they could be overwhelmed by large document review cases. Therefore, developing an understanding of document review is very important.[8]

It is the overwhelming volume of data that we create, and not the litigation rules, that drive the need for document review. If some law firms do not embrace strategies to deal with larger document review projects, the question for them is not if, but when, they will struggle to do a competent document review project for their clients.

3. The emergence of document review: early challenges and lessons learned

There are some lawyers still practising today who remember the file drawers and boxes of papers stored in warehouses for the very large cases. In those days, it was much easier to find evidence if filing was done accurately and record managers were used properly, or to lose evidence because paper does not get shared as much as electronic records. Today we create much more evidence, and record management systems to store information have been overwhelmed, allowing evidence to disappear due to the challenges of maintaining and tracking so much information. Our smartphones, computers and tablets all create records every time we use them. This is unlike the old days, when a secretary had to type up a record and then put it

"Our smartphones, computers and tablets all create records every time we use them."

somewhere after the attorney reviewed the documents and they were used. Given the onslaught of data in recent years, there is no way to avoid review when embroiled in a legal dispute. This has brought two constellations of challenges for competent document review: human capabilities and hidden quality.

3.1 Not everyone can do document review work
Why do available law firm associates tend to be less adept at larger document review projects? This issue arose in the early days at the beginning of the development of document review as an industry in the United States. It remains a critical issue in much of the world today, especially in emerging and recently emerged legal markets. A lawyer reading this chapter in Vietnam, for example, might gain insights from the mistakes in the United States when my company, for example, first realised that we needed to find dozens or hundreds of attorneys fairly quickly to staff a document review project.

The genesis of many of the mistakes made in document review projects is the myth that anyone can do document review work. It is not viewed as a skill. So why not use available lawyers within a law firm to do the project?

This is how document review developed in the United States. What we learned based on metrics, cost analysis and experiences, is that there is a real art and skill to developing strong review results, ones that are almost impossible to achieve unless the people managing and staffing the review recognise that it takes work, planning and talent to do good review. A corollary message is that larger document reviews that are not thought through completely will eventually cause pain at some point in the process. Your pain point might differ, but there will be pain.

Pain comes in many forms:

- not finishing on time;
- producing documents that are not required in the matter at hand, but which are nevertheless sensitive documents;
- producing documents that a good forensic expert can show are incomplete because conversations have obvious holes in them; and
- spending lots of money.

These are some of the most frequent pains that can emerge in poorly constructed document review projects.

The substantial higher cost of having law firm associates review documents produced the need for a large staffing industry to be created just to review electronic records for law firms. Over time, there became a battle of sorts on how much the law firm had to check the 'first-pass' review done by temporary lawyers. In fact, it gave rise to the concepts of 'first-pass' review and 'second-pass' review. Some clients began to question the need to pay for two reviews when they believed that one pass, if done properly, should be sufficient.[9]

Case study 1: in-house or outsource?
A good case study in good review versus traditional review arose in the first large review I staffed at Legal Network, the first legal staffing company I started. This was in the age before electronic discovery, which came a few years after, but it was a large document review. We partnered with a mid-size Pittsburgh law firm, then with 40 attorneys, with one of the largest law firms in Atlanta, with hundreds of lawyers, on the other side.[10] During the course of the project, my team grew to over 30 attorneys. The seller did what most law firms did back then – and still do today – and found underutilised associates to look over the documents before they turned the documents over to us, representing the buyer. Normally, the seller has an advantage in a complex sale like this, in that they have seen all the original documents and the buyer usually has a smaller window of time to digest the documents and decide if they are paying a fair price. However, our team was able to review the documents in almost real time, given their size, ability to focus

exclusively on this project, and use of technology to build a database to operate the assets that were being acquired. Anyone who saw the review up front was able to see that the seller's law firm, which staffed the review with their own associates, was overwhelmed by its responsibility to review all of this data in a short time. This review experience taught me first-hand why outsourced reviewers can provide a huge advantage in quality over law firm associates who need to add more projects to their time sheet.[11]

In my experience staffing document reviews for two decades, sloppy reviews are typical when they are done by distracted attorneys who are not skilled in document review, and without a dedicated approach for document-intensive projects. These firms struggle to find associates who have time to spare. Those associates might be incredibly bright lawyers, but they usually have other projects at the same time that the lawyers with whom they are working consider to be important projects, even if not as large as the document review project. Pressure from other outside projects can cause the focus on the document review project to be diminished. This, in turn, causes the decisions associates make when reviewing documents to be inconsistent with decisions they make on similar documents at different points in the review. It also makes it harder to finish the review on time.

Another type of diminished focus is caused by the associates themselves, who recognise that, by working on document review projects, they cannot impress the partners who determine their future career path at the law firm. As a result, while assigned to a document review project, many of them seek other tasks or opportunities to work on other matters. Becoming a partner in a law firm requires associates to show the partners that they are good enough lawyers to be promoted. Document review does not provide the same opportunity to shine as does an individual research project, presenting motions in court, or drafting documents.

My theory at the time as I started trying to educate law firms on how to improve document review was that turnover on document review projects handled by law firms internally tends to be much higher than those firms are comfortable to admit to their clients. Turnover is even greater than when using an outside agency whose attorneys are usually also looking for new projects.

"Pressure from other outside projects can cause the focus on the document review project to be diminished."

Case study 2: large-scale outsourcing and internal financial politics

In 2002, a partner at a Pittsburgh law firm, with several hundred attorneys, asked me to help convince his client to use contracted attorneys in a pharmaceutical matter. We drafted a bid and provided references for what was supposed to be a 10-lawyer project lasting six months. That calculation was wrong and it turned into the largest document review project in the United States, eventually with over 240 contract lawyers working for a five-year period.[12]

Three months into the project, the review team had grown to 60 attorneys, and relations between the law firm partner who was supervising the matter and our team deteriorated. The opportunity that the law firm and our firm had to make a great deal of money created an atmosphere of distrust between supposed partners on a project. Our external team of attorneys now generated much of the law firm's profits.[13]

Fair treatment was the paramount concern of the review team. They were all working on the tenth floor of the building, 30 floors beneath the law firm's main offices. It might have seemed like the same firm, but these floors did not even share the same elevator bank. None of the partners ever came to visit them. When I discovered this, I asked whether the main partner in the matter should come down, talk to the team, and thank them for the first time. I was advised by my former employee, who had been hired away to manage the project, that it would likely scare the entire team, who had not met him during the first four years of the project.

Being marginalised in this way definitely impacted them. This happens on large document review projects, and it happens to reviewers over time, too, in markets that have developed document review attorneys' services to rent out lawyers. It is almost impossible to stand out even if you do a great job. The long-term projects do offer some promotions and additional responsibilities, but somehow showing this to the next client on your resume is almost impossible to capture.

Moreover, in the markets where I have experience, no one who went to law school ever planned to do document review as their job. So depression is sometimes some of the baggage brought by review attorneys, especially ones who have lost their jobs at law firms. If they do not have clients that they can bring with them, they find that other large law firms usually develop their staff from new attorneys hired out of law school. Understanding the emotional

"Moreover, in the markets where I have experience, no one who went to law school ever planned to do document review as their job."

needs of contract attorneys can help a client, law firm or staffing agency avoid the many problems that can easily occur.[14]

One of the biggest concerns – and often a source of complaint – of review attorneys is being able to make the same amount of money as others on the project because they are all doing the same type of work. Having other staffing agencies offering a single dollar more per hour to try to recruit away my team was a never-ending headache for us.

4. Hidden quality

Hidden quality has been another huge problem for an external provider of document review services. Some reviewers in the pharmaceutical project described above thought that they were better than others on the project, and many disagreed vehemently with the coding of their quality control attorney, or QCer.[15]

Document review remains a thankless job even today, but recognising that some reviewers are better than others at the same type of work led to some of my biggest successes in the field decades later, when I built the first document review test used in the industry. Recognising there is a never-ending battle to achieve a uniform review approach requires substantial effort. Talent alone will not get a team on the same page but real-time communication can.[16]

Management and quality control are very real challenges that take up a lot of a manager's time. These issues are explored in greater detail in two sections later in this chapter. The lesson here is that successful management of a document review is much more complicated than just finding available attorneys to look at documents. That concept is fundamental, but almost no one who has not worked on a review project has any concept of it.

Hidden quality in document review has a corollary – all reviewers have roughly the same quality, but differences can be significant. Just ask anyone who has done quality control reviews on document review projects. They will probably talk your ear off on the differences among different reviewers. I found out how hard it is to promote higher quality reviewers years later at my last document review company, which deployed a document review test I had built. It used reviewer metrics to determine who to put on a project. As part of that software, we would sometimes input the speed of the document review attorney as a variable, and we could even embed the rating of the reviewer.[17] Law firms and corporate law departments that are considering outsourced document review providers should ask what, if any, testing is administered to their reviewers.

So, if you are new to review, understand that there are quality differences among different reviewers. The other important insight is that quality alone does not make a review team great. It is a good starting point, but, as will be discussed later in this chapter, even with high quality, there is more to the story of improving document review.

Another way to look at the hidden quality issue is to consider that an attorney coding alone on a computer screen may perceive things differently to what a colleague might see in the same document. The correct coding answer sometimes might be grey, not black-and-white. Inconsistency can be a huge problem. The managers whom I employed told me how hard they had to work to re-review documents to get the results to be coherent.[18]

Case study 3: quality and the competition for talent
In one large document review,[19] the external project leaders, who managed the team and did the quality control work, received special treatment from their law firm customer and were paid more money. They told me that there were leaders who were treated better and paid more money. For example, they received special meals and key fobs to securely enter the review centre at any time and were assigned office space instead of cubicles. Of particular interest, they were personally recruited by the law firm on the project. This is because the law firm was not allowed to charge a mark-up on the document reviewers put on the project, but it could mark up for the quality control reviews. In short, the law firm recruited these quality control people on their own, using online recruiting and advertisement, thus competing against an agency with extensive skill. Not only were the quality control reviewers making more money and being treated much better, but it appeared these reviewers were not as competent as the first-pass reviewers recruited by the agency.

The lesson learned in this example is an important one. The economic impact of document review can be substantial. Adding outside reviewers to reduce the costs and to deal with a fast-growing volume of electronic records can create competition for talent in the market. In the United States, that battlefield expanded to include the software vendors who supply the processing tools to capture and see the electronic records and the databases in which to do the reviews. Because there is seldom a lot of news in the public domain about legal projects, usually only the law firms and the technology providers even know that there is a document review opportunity.

Different law firms treat this economic battle differently. Some look at document review as being a less sophisticated part of legal practice and something for which they do not want to bill their clients. Others look at it as an opportunity to make money quickly and in large quantities. Given the fact that it is an inefficient market, ethical issues can arise which can impact the quality of the review work. This case study is an example of economics getting in the way of building a quality environment for the project.

As discussed in the next section of this chapter, document review technology can help avoid some of these mistakes by speeding up a review and making it more accurate.

5. Using technology to improve document review and lower its costs

Over the past 20 years, as bodies of relevant documentary information in litigation and major commercial transactions became bigger, and the need for fast, cost-efficient, high-quality document review has become even more important in the legal services industry worldwide, like many in the field I have begun to explore and adapt advanced technology to reduce the costs of document review and to improve and sustain consistently high levels of quality.

5.1 The evolution of advanced technology

The emergence of advanced technology, such as predictive coding, was an evolutionary process. The main steps in the process included:

- greater awareness and understanding of the potential of technology to introduce and support dramatic improvements in the document review process;[20]
- working with trial judges to encourage them to allow litigants to use more technology in functions such as document review;[21]
- the development of software that built an intersection between predictive coding and document review;[22] and
- the use of meta data behind each document to allow an attorney to analyse the case based on the relevant electronic records.[23]

Case study 4: *Global Aerospace*

The *Global Aerospace* case[24] demonstrated how predictive coding could work if used correctly. The litigation involved hangars that stored many expensive aeroplanes at Dulles Airport, near Washington DC, and which collapsed during a heavy snowfall. We used a predictive coding tool and had an attorney review 5,000 documents from a collection of about 1.5 million records. Based on that review, the computer then predicted that 140,000 records were useful to the case. Once documents that were part of the email threads were added back, 200,000 documents were produced. The client saved lots of money in the process and the sampling statistics we used when studying the documents we were producing – and, importantly, what was being left behind – predicted that we were finding 82% of the documents with minimal effort. By contrast, US government-sponsored research done by the Text Retrieval Conference (TREC) to evaluate computer-assisted review's accuracy found that, in their research groups, document review through physical eyeballs on every document identified only 68% of the responsive records review.[25] This case demonstrated how predictive coding could produce a highly efficient review.[26]

So, how good are humans at reviewing documents? The best way to determine this is to survey your own coding and have an experienced 'judge' determine how accurately they were reviewed. If you reviewed 1 million records, a random survey of 600 coded documents would give you 95% confidence that whatever your judge found was within ±5% of the result for all one million records. The problem is that few attorneys who conducted the reviews ever know how well they did.

The best person to ask whether the reviewing attorneys are accurate, without doing a formal survey, is the attorney who performs quality control checks on the results and tries to clean

"The best person to ask whether the reviewing attorneys are accurate, without doing a formal survey, is the attorney who performs quality control checks on the results and tries to clean up errors."

up errors. Otherwise, you might have to rely on the studies like TREC. We used TREC results in the *Global Aerospace* case to promise that we would stop using the software to train the software after it predicted more than 75% recall, on the theory that then we would be doing at least as good as a human review. We achieved a rate of approximately 82% and stopped our training of the software after 5,000 documents.

Case study 5: *Garlock* bankruptcy case

The *Garlock* bankruptcy case[27] was a bigger opportunity to combine technology and review, using a national and remote team of reviewers relying on my testing software. I was appointed as the Special Master for electronic discovery to assist the bankruptcy divisions of the Federal District Courts for the Western District of Pennsylvania and the District of Delaware with redacting over one million records of claimants in 11 asbestos cases that had settled and created trust funds to pay out millions of dollars to victims.

The company Garlock claimed that many victims were accusing every company sued for asbestos contamination as the source of their illnesses. It sought the records containing personal health information for the large trust funds that were supervised by these two courts. This required redacting the first four digits of each claimant's social security record before producing the medical records. The problem was the social security numbers were all over the place. We had so many to redact that it was almost impossible to predict how many reviewers it would take to manually redact the social security numbers as had been ordered by a Federal District Court judge. Some documents were even named based on the social security numbers. Many of the documents were scanned records from the earliest days of the first use of scanners. Many social security numbers were written by hand. It was a very messy collection.

I picked a new technology which sorted records based on glyph technology. In simple terms, the software looked at a picture of each document to group similar documents in piles. A search tool to find and highlight 10-digit numbers was built into the software. Thus, similar forms – regardless of whether they were in PDF, Word, WordPerfect formats, or a form that had been scanned and completed by hand – would be grouped together as exact matches, even if they were slightly different. Had we used traditional search tools, similar documents would have been treated as different records. By finding all documents that looked similar and grouping them together, our theory was we could quickly redact documents because our reviewer could look to the same areas in each cluster of similar documents and do a bulk redacting of social security numbers.[28]

We finished the project right at the trial deadline with a few days to spare. What could have been a multi-million dollar review actually cost approximately $80,000, not including my Special Master fees, because we leveraged technology with an outstanding review team.[29]

The most important message is no one needs to get hung up on how the technology they pick actually works. Statistics and sampling will allow you to understand whether the tool is finding or leaving behind the documents that should be found. There is no such thing as perfection in review. However, sampling is a wonderful tool that a law firm can use to review 400–600 random documents and form an opinion on whether the predictive coding is working well enough.

Case study 6: Can you trust the other side's technology?
Around this time, I was asked by a leading plaintiff firm in a class action to advise them in their action against a large telecommunications carrier for securities law violations and making misleading statements to boost their stock price. The parties had agreed to use predictive coding. My job was to keep an eye on the defendant's use of predictive coding to make sure that their process would result in a fair production to the plaintiff. It seems that my client did not trust the defendants.

The opposing counsel doing the review were from one of the largest law firms in the world. One of the vendors whom I had closely examined during the process explained in detail how their system worked but did not understand or could not explain why their software worked. He could not do anything to explain the reports we were receiving. It was an eye-opening experience. The first batch of documents, which were coded to train the software on what to seek, resulted in sampling results better than what we accepted in *Global Aerospace*. Knowing the software was only finding what it was fed, we insisted that they work longer to try to find more documents to train the software, in order not to miss documents that might be buried and were not similar to the documents used to train the software.

A funny thing happened. The sampling numbers they were revealing to us showing the software they were using dropped a full 10 percentage points over a two-month period. What was going wrong? We asked to see the documents that were being coded by an associate at the law firm to see if there was inconsistent coding. Inconsistent coding is the enemy of computer-assisted review. Given the small number of documents coded at this stage, I was sure that the associate on this project was doing other projects at the same time as the coding on this project. I rationalised that if they would show us how they coded a small number of documents, we could work together with them and agree how to fix any inconsistent coding errors that were confusing the predictive coding software. We then could use the predictive coding for the rest of the several million documents needed to be completed and could have recommended the documents that should be produced.

The other side disagreed, perhaps not wanting to be embarrassed by coding a handful of documents incorrectly or just to delay the case further. They fought not to share any of their limited coding and instead opted to give up on predictive coding and do a manual review of about 80% of the document pool, which was several million records. So much for having new technology work on a project to save money and speed up review! This added a huge cost for the defendant and caused more delays for my client to receive documents. It was an eye-opening experience, and it showed me that even a very smart lawyer at one of the best law firms can mess up a predictive coding review by not coding consistently.

"Inconsistent coding is the enemy of computer-assisted review."

5.2 The emergence of predictive coding

By 2009, technology people were starting to think more seriously about predictive coding. Predictive coding is a lot like the spam filter in your email box. If you open it, you will see lots of emails which on their face look like junk: emails about miracle drugs for sale; foreign women who want to meet you; and ways to regrow hair and make other body parts work better. Occasionally you will see an email that you want to read, which is not spam; this proves that the spam filter is not perfect. So, in response you can code the desired email as not being spam, and the software learns from your coding and accepts that email address as a verified sender in the future. Likewise, you can also mark emails which you did not want to receive as spam, and in the future the spam filter will do a better job of stopping those emails from reaching your inbox. How did the software know to prevent which emails from reaching your inbox? The software designers used common emails and topics in emails that users marked as spam to predict if an email is spam.

Predictive coding works the same way in a lawsuit or an investigation. The only difference is, unlike spam, it is impossible for a software engineer to know upfront what a useful document looks like for a lawsuit and what an irrelevant document looks like. That is where lawyers reviewing documents and coding them as useful or not useful helps to train the software how to code the remaining documents, which have not been reviewed, and predict what is useful and what is not.

The three immediately preceding case studies illustrate the conservative nature of lawyers and how reluctant they are to try new tools. They show how using technology can be a key component in the most effective reviews. New technology can be intimidating, but technology will always be faster and cheaper than manual review alone. Lawyers frequently overlook how the quality of the review teams can be critically important to making the technology work as designed. Technology alone does not work out of the box to solve legal problems. The more we did remote reviews, the clearer it became that having talented teams also reduced the amount of clean-up work which most reviews require. Having a talented team is irreplaceable.[30]

So how is document review done with predictive coding? This is too technical a question for any single person to answer. Technology has no doubt changed since I stopped doing review projects, but according to my friends in the industry the basics still hold true. You can always use a sampling of what the software deems to be relevant to the case and, equally important, a sample of what you determine is not responsive to determine if your technology is working reliably.

Sampling can be done not only with computer-assisted review but also to deploy reviewers to tackle batches or data sets and make decisions on whether to look more deeply into a data set.

Therefore, if you understand a little bit about how to sample data, you should be comfortable using any new predictive technology. The challenge is that many lawyers chose law to avoid maths, but there are enough lawyers who do understand basic statistics. My advice is to have someone at your legal organisation or with your technology vendor help you to understand how to sample a data set to confirm that your review is heading in the right direction.

5.3 The critical importance of good people

Good lawyers are critically important.

Case study 7: The Oracle study

In 2013, Patrick Oot was conducting research with the E-Discovery Institute and partnered with the legal department at Oracle to study how different tools performed with the same data set. Oracle wanted to pick its predictive coding software vendor based on these results, and anyone who wanted to win Oracle's business entered this contest. The interesting thing was that, in some instances, different entrants used the same software tools. However, the same software tools would sometimes perform well and sometimes poorly with the same data. The only difference was the review teams who were using the same tools. Different people see different things when they view the same documents.

By 2014, predictive coding was slowly gaining momentum. More and more people wanted to be experts.[31]

6. Location, health and quality issues in document review projects

As noted previously in this chapter, document reviewers often do not agree on what a document says and how it impacts a lawsuit. For that reason, the quality of a review requires the most talented document review attorneys that can be found.

I was always interested in how to find the best reviewers and the challenges I saw from doing review for a project in a single review location. There are many lawyers who are looking for full-time jobs or who have law practices which are sometimes less busy than usual. Wouldn't it be better to recruit from the biggest pool of lawyers possible to pick a review team? This had never been done in the United States – at least as the basis for a document review business.

If you accept that document review is a special skill, then you would want to draw from a broad pool of talent. If you never thought of it as a skill, then you would only look for the 10, 20, or however many attorneys you need to show up at your review centre. The best way to do document review is remotely. This is not to say that you cannot do document review in a single market or single location, but remote document review has a number of advantages.

6.1 Responding to a shortage of review talent in a single market

It is impossible for a law firm needing document reviewers to know if their market already has more projects than experienced review attorneys because no one advertises when their pool of review attorneys has dwindled. This was always the argument against trying to staff a substantial case outside of a national commercial centre like Washington DC, New York City or Chicago, in regional markets like Pittsburgh, Minneapolis or Cleveland.[32] The easiest way to assess if a market is thin on review talent is if you are only seeing new attorneys when recruiting for a project and no one with any experience. It is also a real risk when doing on-site reviews when you are asking your review team to show up every day at a physical address.

Even if there isn't a big, talent-consuming case in progress in a single market, the need for specialised talent, in securities law or antitrust law for example, could make it difficult to find more than a handful of these specialists in any one market. For example, most regulatory reviews in the United States tend to be done in Washington, which has some of the most expensive review costs. But if you looked around the rest of the country, you could assemble a list of attorneys organised by practice area expertise.[33] Allowing the entire project to be staffed with that subject matter expertise, if it is important to the project, could be a huge boost when reading technical documents.

6.2 Shifting work to less expensive markets

Another benefit of remote review is using less expensive review locations from which to recruit talented reviewers.[34] You can deal with the occasional shortage of review attorneys in a single market and push work to a group of less expensive locations. Similar to a mutual fund for investing, holding a geographically dispersed collection of review attorney displaces some of the risk, such as some of those remote markets not having sufficient numbers of lawyers to staff an entire review. An up-to-date database is required to track where the candidate attorneys are located. In my experience, review attorneys are likely to move to new locations to chase projects or, because they have not established individual career paths, they are not tied to one location.[35]

6.3 Customised and scalable subject-matter driven reviews

An entire team of reviewers with expertise in the subject matter of the case can be recruited across markets (eg, teams of antitrust

"In my experience, review attorneys are likely to move to new locations to chase projects or, because they have not established individual career paths, they are not tied to one location."

lawyers in an antitrust case, or real estate attorneys for due diligence projects in major real estate transactions). This would be impossible to do in any but the largest cities in the United States, and there is nothing to guarantee that those reviewers would be as good as those available from a larger, geographically dispersed, pool of candidates. Highly specialised document review projects often require special skills, such as:

- the ability to use and draw inferences from statistical analyses to determine whether they needed to search for more information to develop a case strategy;
- a very high level of accuracy because the reviewer could be the only one working with a certain type of specialised document; and
- good communication skills with respect to the technical nature of the information in the documents.

This type of analytical review is different from just finding the information to be considered in a case. In many ways, it can be the most powerful form of review because it allows lawyers to put the 'story behind their case' together supported by trustworthy documents. Specialisation could be the eventual direction of document review, much like traditional law firm practice groups with somewhat customised and specialised skill sets. This could help document review gain traction as a specialised field accepted as a professional specialty by attorneys.

6.4 Stop-and-start flexibility in the flow of litigation, document collection or strategy of the case

Because it involves an attorney logging into a computer while at home, sometimes at night, remote document review projects can be stopped and started depending on the processing of data or the posture of the case at that time. This allows considerable flexibility that is lost when attorneys must be physically at a review centre during working hours of the day. It avoids the issue of attorneys needing to be paid for their time at the centre if the review technology goes down for any reason. It is harder to justify not paying someone who has commuted to an office and is ready for work.

But if they are at their home offices, it is less inconvenient to ask them to stop billing the project for their time. It also is easier to manage a remote team during temporary stops or slowdowns in the pace of the case or matter.[36]

6.5 Lifestyle and comfort concerns

The world for most document review attorneys involves living in a city with enough size to support a legal community and a customer base of businesses to create document review projects. Those projects typically do not pay great salaries and have limited duration. A review attorney with uncertain income often lives with a substantial commute to get to the review centre or law firm that has the project. That can add two or more hours to their day, such as many other professionals face.

Given the grind of the work, it is helpful to let someone work at home. No one could ever build a review centre as comfortable as someone's home. Free coffee and a good chair only go so far. A person's home office will in most cases be more comfortable to do review work. Someone who is exhausted, or has to deal with a crisis with the kids or sickness, or just has something else to do can always make up the hours later in the day or into the evening. Over and over again, my company's reviewers said how much they loved this environment.

6.6 The ability of law to reduce its carbon footprint

Remote document reviews make sense for sustainability reasons.[37]

The carbon footprint of remote review has two drivers. The first is eliminating doing review in an office building. Office buildings historically have not been designed with environmental costs in mind. These costs are typically buried in the lease with utilities being spread across tenants. They are hidden, but they are real. Approximately 40% of the world's energy consumption comes from office buildings, with most of it coming from lighting, heating, cooling and air conditioning.[38]

a) Air conditioning and energy costs

These costs are even higher for air conditioning in review centres because reviewers sitting in close proximity to each other with computer equipment running makes these rooms hot.[39] As global warming accelerates, air conditioning use increases, so the problem is getting worse. In doing larger document review projects in an older building, we used to bring fans in to cool the rooms because the temperatures were so uncomfortable.

Unlike a typical office layout, reviewers are often crammed into expensive office buildings because it was assumed by many review companies that they had to be close to the law firms that hired them. Even in a newer building, which might not need fans because the air conditioning does a better job of keeping the temperature cooler, the costs are substantial. Moreover, it is important to keep the reviewers comfortable in their close workspaces, so air conditioning is used more than is normally used in office buildings.

Contrast this with the fact that reviewers already have a house or apartment and are already paying for their own air conditioning and heating. Houses and apartments have a better opportunity to be designed to be eco-efficient because the occupant sees a bill and can adjust the energy usage to economise, if desired. It is not a hidden cost. And without many workstations being close by, the room at home does not need to be cooled to the same degree as a review centre.

b) Commuting

The second driver is the commute to work, which usually requires fossil fuels. Because car types are different and cities have different commuting distances and conditions, it is an impossible exercise to measure the financial and environmental costs precisely. However, some rough modelling is possible. If your average commute is 20 miles (32.20 km) and your car had a fuel mileage rating of 20 mpg, you would burn two gallons (7.57 litres) of fuel on your daily commute. Assuming that a gallon of petrol produces 18.07 pounds (8.20 kg) of carbon,[40] one day of commuting would produce more than 72 pounds (approximately 32.80 kg) of carbon.

A basic review project, with 10 attorneys doing review five days per week for three weeks, would produce approximately 10,842 pounds (4,918 kg) of carbon – more than 10 US tonnes – just driving to and from the review centre. Think of all the document review projects done in the United States and around the world.[41]

"There are lots of benefits to testing, but the real secret is rating attorneys at the end of the project, on the work they produced, and not the test results."

6.7 What's the big deal? Has COVID-19 pushed everything to 'remote'?

Today the world is different from many of the case studies in this chapter. We have COVID-19. In the early days of document review, we only had to deal with influenza, which could temporarily make review centres super-spreading centres, or the occasional hurricane hitting a centre with damage that could be repaired.

As a result – in part due to the technology-driven shift in the cost-benefit equation and more recently due to the COVID-19 pandemic of 2020 – much if not all review in the United States is now being done remotely. One would expect the same situation in other parts of the world. So why the big sales pitch in this chapter about the benefits of remote review?

Even today, managers in many instances hate remote review. They have to work much harder managing a work day which can last 16–18 hours, with dispersed attorneys logging in to work at different times. In addition, if a remote review is staffed with poor reviewers, and managers cannot personally observe their poor work behaviours, then all remote review does is create a spread-out management mess. I fear today that poor remote review project experiences will cause the review world to revert to some form of the review centre approach once vaccines are available, especially if they can point to a string of bad remote review experiences producing bad results.[42]

COVID-19 is the big deal changer though, and what about the next pandemic? Given all the quality advantages of remote review, what can be the rationale for not doing a remote review? The following sections of this chapter will focus on different objections to remote review and how to resolve them.

7. Using testing to find the best remote review attorneys to interview

If you agree that remote review is a strategy you would like to develop, all the available attorneys who might answer an advertisement could overwhelm you without a way to filter the talent to select the candidates to interview. Giving an attorney 10–20 documents to code is a better way to assess ability than asking in an interview, "Are you a good document review attorney?"

Can a test actually predict who can work for two weeks, show up, follow instructions and finish a job on time and within budgeted costs? The obvious answer is *no*. However, a test gives you data upon which to make a decision and evidence that your team is superior to other document review teams who might be assembled in a particular market. There is also a placebo effect from telling every reviewer picked, "You are an all-star".[43]

There are lots of benefits to testing, but the real secret is rating attorneys at the end of the project, on the work they produced, and not the test results. Like shopping online, it is this history that provides the most comfort in deciding whom to pick for a project. Many law firms and agencies today keep lists as simple as rating attorneys on a one-to-three scale for consideration for future projects. The industry leaders accept prior project work history as one of the most important metrics when evaluating an attorney for a future project.

In emerging legal markets, it may take some time to build up a pool of experienced reviewers. Testing might provide a boost to creating a document review market in your country.

8. Training and communicating with remote reviewers

This was one of the biggest early objections to remote document review. After quality of the reviewer, being able to communicate rapidly and across the entire review team is of paramount importance.

Understanding this solution requires insight into how document review projects normally begin. First the law firm usually prepares a document called a coding protocol, which gives an overview of the case. The best coding protocols also include examples of documents the reviewer might see and how the law firm wants them coded. After the training meeting, batches are given to the review team and they start coding. As quickly as possible, in a well-managed traditional review, the batches are assessed by the lead attorney or quality control attorneys. A follow-up meeting is held and the lead attorney discusses the errors they have found and continues to train the review team so that they may be better informed on how the firm wants the review handled.

The effective use of chat rooms to manage the review versus holding infrequent meetings to manage on-site reviews, offers immediate feedback to questions as they arise and before documents are coded incorrectly.[44] The chat enables all attorneys on the review to see the question as it is asked and give their reaction to it. The lead attorney's response is the final answer, but until that happens at least there is a record of how the review team has assessed the issue. The lead attorneys should watch for questions and be prepared in the first few days to provide feedback.

Case study 8: the chat room

Our company had a high-level regulatory review involving criminal charges for alleged price fixing involving a number of companies. The review was constantly evolving due to changing deadlines and productions to different entities. I discussed the chat room with the associate who was running the review and he said he was open to new techniques, but he wanted traditional meetings as well.

At the first training call the associate wanted to cover some antitrust law. He asked the team if any of the 22 lawyers had antitrust experience. All 22 chatted back they did. I then mentioned that the team had been recruited based on the subject matter of the project. For the next 30 seconds, you could hear the associate thumbing through his presentation on antitrust law to get to the factual part of the training call.

During the call, our team asked questions as they had them. One of the reviewers who typed very fast became the project secretary. At the end of the training, the questions would be asked, and the secretary would record the answers in the chat room.

Two things were accomplished. First, without a single document having been reviewed, the associate now saw his review team as being competent and interested in doing a good job. Second, if we added reviewers, we not only had the training materials ready, but we could show the new team the question-and-answer part of the chat log.

The following week we had our first scheduled meeting. The associate started the call by saying how thrilled he was with the chat feature. In real time, he had been able to answer questions, and so he had little to present to the team except to compliment them on the great job they were doing. I then asked the associate: "What would the impact on productivity have been if the dozens of questions you received before were only now being answered for the first time at this meeting? How much incorrect coding would have been done?"

By communicating in real time, problems are addressed before the documents are reviewed incorrectly. In most reviews, the burden of cleaning up this miscoding at the beginning falls on the quality control attorneys, who use searches to assess if the coding is accurate and if any documents have been missed.

8.1 Communication dynamics and chat tools

There are other communication dynamics at play. When explaining chatting tools to clients who questioned their effectiveness, I asked them to close their eyes and imagine they are doing a review: "You are in the middle of a 75-page document. You have twenty codes to apply. It is a technical and boring document. Suddenly, you hear your colleagues talking about a document they have a question about. Is that good communication?"

The answer is *yes* for the reviewers who have the question because you want questions to be asked. However, it is ineffective because it distracts attorneys who are in the middle of coding. They might be in a coding zone and highly focused on their task and might not want to talk just then. After reviewing documents, they can look at the chat log and see what issue was raised.

Secondly, who should get the question: the review attorney's neighbour in the centre, or the attorney who is overseeing the case? Law firms often have a very junior person acting as a quasi-babysitter monitoring the room. Very often they cannot answer questions, but they will compile them into an issue log and share them with the lead attorney. Using a chat room puts the trial team and lead attorney into the coding room with real-time eyes and ears, regardless of where anyone is located.

The chat helps to build reviewer team morale. Often reviewers will not know some of the other review attorneys on a project. Seeing how the team communicates during a project provides a mechanism to encourage good habits and professionalism in a review team. If you are trying to build an all-star team culture for the reviewers, chat builds relationships across the review team across different cities.[45] Chat works with attorneys who are talented and who want to be respected for the talent they bring to the project.

Even so, some law firms might still be suspicious or sceptical about chat tools. One preeminent trial law firm that I met was horrified. They said the last thing they wanted is a record of their review team's conversations. One can only speculate why. They were used to having and seeing reviewers in a room. Were they concerned that the law firm's client might see the chat log?[46]

My response is that if you do not promote talking, how can you train the team effectively to be on the same page quickly? From operations and quality perspectives, chat is a useful tool.

Case study 9: the value of a chat log

At least one law firm liked having a record of the chat and chose us for a project because we used it. It enabled them to dispel any concerns that they did not do a diligent job on the review. They had evidence they could present, something no one else was offering at the time.

The first highly complex review we did using the chat involved 80 attorneys. We were asked just before Thanksgiving, the second biggest holiday in the United States, to staff a project that involved car warranty complaint software not working. The regulatory agency noticed that a vehicle manufacturer had zero reported warranty claims over a period of several years. This agency had done very little enforcement until a spate of lawsuits occurred. Now they were auditing compliance records and this result stood out. The agency immediately fined our client $7,000 a week until they could determine why the software our client used to assist with customer complaints stopped forwarding those complaints to the regulators for several years.

This was a very complicated case because what might be a serious defect was hard to discern factually. Our team was spread across the United States and would debate back and forth about the text messages and records they reviewed. They did not always agree on what to do, but I was proud to evaluate the record. I knew that even if we made a mistake in categorising a particular customer exchange, no one could question how hard our team worked to uncover what were safety defects that should have been reported versus what might have been just a bad paint job on a vehicle.

We finished the review over a remarkable eight-day period and also fully staffed this project on the Monday following Thanksgiving, the same day other document review and staffing agencies were only just responding to the frantic message they received from the law firm the previous Wednesday afternoon.

8.2 Which chat tool to use?

This is not a critical issue; however, I have always advocated for a tool that is outside of the review platform. This allows partners at the law firm to participate in discussions and see the chat which will help to develop confidence in the skills of the review team. Most law firm partners have never logged into any of the complicated review software programs being used.[47]

Today there are many encrypted chat tools that could be used.[48] The only caveat is to make sure the tool offers adequate encryption and the review team has administrative control over who to add and remove from the chat room. Projects change in scope and size, and people join and leave projects for a variety of reasons. So being able to change who can read the chat record is very important.

9. Quality control

Quality is really important to a review team.[49] There are several ways to assure it.

The best time to do a quality control review is at the beginning of the project before many documents have been coded incorrectly. Reviewing a complete set of documents in the first batch of

"The best time to do a quality control review is at the beginning of the project before many documents have been coded incorrectly."

documents seen allows a quality control attorney to make sure that the reviewer is following instructions provided by the outside law firm. Waiting until the end of the project to do a quality control review loses the ability to teach a review team how to do the first pass review correctly before they make mistakes.[50]

Much quality control is built around meetings, which are easier in an on-site review. Chat tools really help quality control in remote reviews. A mistake can be identified, and the entire review team can be told by chat in real time, as opposed to waiting for a time to meet while the team to continues to make the same coding mistake.

The end of the project is, of course, a significant time for quality control. In the United States, where the concept of privileged documents applies to lawyer communications with clients, much effort is spent trying to find privileged conversations and putting together the threads of conversations that might have been broken during the processing of the data. A good quality control attorney will use the tools available to do powerful analytical searches and then add bulk tags. They will look for anomalies in the coding such as: 'broken families', when parts of an email thread are coded as privileged but other parts are not; documents that are missing coding; and documents tagged as 'technical issue'. However, this clean-up can also result in hiding the identity of the member of the team who incorrectly coded the document in the first place.

The final point about quality control is it takes a different set of skills than the speed desired in a first-pass review. Methodical but accurate reviewers can often be outstanding quality control attorneys but only average first-pass reviewers. However, the attorneys with blazing review speed and substandard reading comprehension skills might not perform well on quality control projects. How the review team is organised is another nuance of designing better review projects.

Quality assurance is important because if you can avoid making mistakes with the first-pass review with better reviewers and better communications, you can sharply reduce the amount of clean-up work a quality control attorney has to do later. Quality control attorneys are usually paid much more than the first-pass review team, and poor quality in the first-pass review not only lengthens the time frame to finish a project, but it adds to the cost. There seem to be enough great reviewers on most projects, albeit in small numbers, so they can clean up many of the mistakes in first-pass review. However, it is stressful work to run searches and look for common errors, usually done under time pressures. This is also an opportunity for review companies to make more money and profits by charging a higher rate for quality control work.[51]

10. Maintaining data security
This is the big issue in remote review and whether it is better than on-site review. Another chapter in this book addresses cybersecurity, so this discussion will not go into as much detail. There are answers available to address this concern about data security, and there might be some cases where on-site review is ultimately selected because clients are fearful of data being seen outside of a review centre.

- The data started as electronic. In many cases, it was already emailed once outside of a company. Why should this particular data be locked down more than the other data which is being created by the company and law firm outside of the review centre?
- The professionals who are receiving the data to review can be licensed attorneys. In my experience, licensed attorneys offer another layer of protection, ie, the reviewer can lose the license to practise law if they mishandle a client's record.
- There is usually a record of metadata kept on any record that any review attorney touches during the review. If a particular document or documents are released, it would be easy to question the attorney who reviewed it.
- Time is money on a document review case. Because review attorneys are looking at 60–100 documents every hour, there is no time to stop and ponder a document's value outside of the lawsuit. If an attorney slows down, that is easy to spot based on their speed metrics. Most documents are not smoking guns, which incidentally is one more reason in favour of remote review. A dispute with a local company might create something newsworthy to accidentally talk about at dinner with a spouse, but outside of that market, it might be something no one cares about.
- Even in a review centre, there is nothing stopping someone from sneaking a camera in to photograph documents. It is impossible to keep all risks at zero, even with on-site reviews.
- The genie comes out of the bottle the minute a document is reviewed. Once someone sees a document, they have the knowledge the document exists. That knowledge is always a risk in both on-site and remote reviews.
- The biggest risk is having someone mediocre read the document. A dedicated remote team of outstanding review attorneys are constantly in demand for projects. The nuances of any document they see fades in weeks and especially when they move on to another project.
- The more you lock down the reviewers, the more you marginalise them and lose the benefits of treating them as professionals.[52]

Finally, there are data security tools that provide solutions. You can double-authenticate a review attorney every time they log in, using a cellular phone number or email address to obtain a special verification code. The data can sit on secure servers and be locked down so that the reviewer can review only the image of the document but does not keep a copy on the local computer. There are technical ways to turn a computer into a monitor solely accessing a secure server.

There is often some trade-off on speed with more security tools in place. Review attorneys may have trouble logging into a complex system or may forget login codes. All of these issues can be managed. With chat tools, login issues can be handled by the team helping each other, which is another benefit of having an external chat tool available.

11. Respecting the team pays big performance dividends
Even with the best available reviewers and real-time communications, problems may still arise. Review is a messy world and to use a colourful but cleaned-up phrase, 'excrement flows downhill'. Whenever there are problems, it is usually easy to blame the lowest skilled professional on the project. In our world, this is the document review team. The following case study illustrates a good way to circle back to not only treat the review team fairly but going even further and supporting them when there is a challenge.

Case study 10: having the team's back
This case study involves two projects.

The first was a very high-profile project involving security clearance which took over two months to obtain. There were approximately 12,000 documents and we budgeted three reviewers. When one quit during the security process, we were forced to attempt the project with two reviewers.

Several weeks in, the numbers were not good. It appeared that the reviewers were processing only 15 documents per hour. My entire company including my co-CEO turned immediately on these two outstanding reviewers and told the client they were never going to hire these two again and apologised. I took another approach. I talked to both of the reviewers and understood very quickly that they were reviewing in most instances 150-page documents, which were much longer than average documents and contained technical real-estate finance terminology. We were also using a new remote processing tool which few people had used before. In addition, the coding protocol on which they had been trained had been changed after the first few days of the project.

After accounting for those variables, I estimated their output was substantially above average and wrote a two-page memo to the law firm and the government regulatory agency defending the team. This was not my client nor my project, but I knew the two reviewers very well and that two of the best were working on the project. Due to security issues, it was impossible to add another reviewer or two to help them meet the deadline. Instead, these reviewers averaged 15 hours per day, and while their documents per day increased only marginally, they finished the review on time due to their perseverance and commitment to the project. The entire remote leadership team all recognised that I had stood up to the client, tech vendor and our internal management team who had caved in to a client accusation.[53]

A second project where I had to defend the review team involved a 'top-five' law firm which was notoriously hard to work with because they demanded perfection of themselves and everyone who worked with them. The technology firm was using a new approach in trying to predict privileged documents. The problem was that the rethreading they did basically changed the quality control work our lead attorney was doing and erased it, leaving the entire pool of privileged documents to review again.

There was poor communication with the vendor. Our outstanding attorney was almost beside herself. A few documents were produced, and we all got yelled at. After researching the problem, including the chat logs, I wrote a memo congratulating everyone for attempting a new workflow, but pointed out the technology had destroyed our ability to do quality control work. I also pointed out a safe harbour rule passed to protect privileged documents from being produced. It offered free protection because it was widely recognised how hard in an electronic age it is to catch all privileged documents. The courts wanted to encourage litigants to experiment with new technology and not be punished for it. In the end we gave a small discount and the technology company gave a much larger discount because the end result had not been perfect. The law firm ultimately considered our review work to have been outstanding, recognising that the error had been because of the technology company. They continued working with us on other projects. Again, the review team knew I was going to recognise their talents and not blame them if there was an issue on the review without first researching everything that happened.

12. Using metrics to recruit in an existing review business

In most agencies, recruiters pick who will be on a review project, often based on who responds quickest to an advertisement. Metrics are never considered. After some time, some reviewers show loyalty and get picked more frequently.[54] Loyalty is important, but the recruiter often has no idea of how the reviewer actually performed on a project, especially if an outside law firm was the client. The quality control attorneys are often good sources about who did the best and fastest review work.

How this is achieved will depend on the circumstances of each review project. Once that data-driven approach is used, recruiting becomes much easier, and the quality of the review gets increasingly better.[55]

13. Labour laws and taxes

How review attorneys are treated for employment purposes is an issue to be thoroughly considered. Document review projects can be very short in duration, and they are staffed by lawyers. Thus, there are many good arguments against having to employ workers for these types of projects.[56]

In different parts of the world, you must examine labour laws closely. For example, in Brazil there is a 90-day probationary period for all workers to be hired and terminated without paying any unemployment-related fees. This would be adequate for most document review projects. Other countries, like Mexico, are notorious for accepting contractor relationships without much scrutiny from the government. By the reviewing labour laws in any country, a well-thought-out contract with the review attorneys can be created to defend against claims that an employment relationship has been created. This defence is made even stronger by working remotely with the reviewer's own equipment, having them setting their own hours, and allowing them to take other projects without being punished. Given how high employment taxes can be in different parts of the world, this is something worth evaluating closely. In addition, requiring payroll tax collection in a country like the United States, which has federal, state and sometimes local taxes, would make it administratively challenging to pay a national remote review team if they were considered to be employees.

14. Technical configuration of review space

Remote reviews, rather than reviews conducted in a review centre, are usually preferable, but if a review centre is needed, it should be configured to promote productivity and quality.

A review centre should have the ability to separate space between reviews. Having modules that can be separated allows for different configurations. In addition, security fobs to close access to different rooms and areas, as well as security cameras, are very important.

Adding amenities like free coffee and a place where reviewers can go

"Remote reviews, rather than reviews conducted in a review centre, are usually preferable, but if a review centre is needed, it should be configured to promote productivity and quality."

to take phone calls and have some privacy makes the work environment more bearable. Occasional doughnuts or pizza gatherings also go a long way towards keeping the reviewers feeling appreciated.

If a law firm or client are going to visit on-site, they often need a private conference room or a place to work separately from the review team. This enables them to take phone calls that may be unrelated to the project and also to talk about the project without being overheard by the rest of the review team.

Name cards on the review cubicles can also help. They enable a better control mechanism to make sure everyone is present and allow review managers to find reviewers if they do not know them. This seems like a small problem, but with different projects and different review teams, sometimes it is necessary to know who is present and where someone sits in order to manage the review team.

Access to public transport is a huge plus when creating a review centre. In competitive markets, reviewers may leave projects if it is difficult to find transport to where the review is being done.

One benefit of on-site review is that physical documents are sometimes still a part of the review. It is not impossible to have a mixture of on-site review and remote review, but it makes sense to keep the documents under the control of the law firm or client.

The most common form of review involves neither of these approaches, but simply using empty conference rooms or office space and doing the review as an *ad hoc* project. This can certainly work, but internet access must be adequate. For long-term assignments, the comfort and workspaces of the review attorneys should not be a secondary consideration. This is the main reason why some review services lease dedicated configured review centres in the United States and other parts of the world.

Case study 11: outfitting the technology kit
There are some things which should be in place for any type of review, whether remote or at a review centre.

The first is a dual monitor set up. I would ask all remote review attorneys to invest in a large second monitor. This could even be a flat screen television. Because of the need to look at open documents, coding panels to input the appropriate codes, and a chat application, a dual monitor reduces or eliminates the need to scroll back and forth on a page and keep more applications unnecessarily open. With a dual monitor, the reviewer can have everything available to see without having to open and close applications.[57]

The second is that there must be enough bandwidth to load data and do the review quickly. Interestingly, because of video streaming services like Netflix, home offices often have faster download times than review centres where many reviewers may share the same bandwidth. The first remote review I staffed after *Garlock*[58] was with an accounting firm and international law firm in Texas. The reviewers started on-site with two remote reviewers I added to the team. We found immediately that the remote reviewers were more effective, so much so that the rest of the team asked to be allowed to do remote review. Based on the metrics, the law firm and the client agreed. One factor was the quality of the two off-site reviewers. However, the main reason was the PowerPoint files and other large documents did not load as quickly in the review centre the client had set up. This is why dedicated review centres should have T-1 lines to provide more review throughput to share bandwidth with other reviewers without slowing the work.

15. Flexible customised responses to novel situations
Some of the projects in which I have participated were amazing and serve as outstanding case studies in the flexibility and responsiveness that outsourced document review teams can deliver to law firms and clients.

Case study 12: Remote 'hurricane review' saved the day in Florida

Here is a marketing email I wrote describing one of the most amazing projects I have ever seen.

We recently staffed a seemingly impossible review which we completed; normally done in 60 days but we did in a compressed 15-day period. We did 3 reviews during this time in the same project at different intervals. It was a lot like driving a Maserati because our proprietary ReviewRight recruiting and management software allows us to ramp up and down with talented reviewers almost on demand.

THE FACTS: 'Starting the Engine': In this case, an AmLaw-5 firm used our Maserati, our proprietary ReviewRight software and process, to staff 100 attorneys on-site in Florida on a large on-site 2nd request antitrust review using Predictive Coding. The strategy was to review only for privilege and rely on predictive coding to determine responsiveness with lower review costs. The review strategy had to change and add a new review team when it was discovered that there were 300,000 new unreviewed documents which predictive coding had not been used on with only 7 days left in the review

2nd REVIEW: 'Hitting the Accelerator': We deployed almost 200 remote attorneys that weekend 24 hours after the call on the 300,000 documents and finished early with high quality responsiveness coding, redactions, a full privilege log prepared by the Florida team and performed QC.

3rd REVIEW: 'Taking the Final Turn Going Really Fast': Then after the project ended and the review team had been sent home for 3 days, it was realised there was a need to review over 100,000 new unreviewed documents over the final weekend. The same day within hours, we mobilised 100 remote attorneys who started reviewing immediately and hit the deadline with 52 minutes to spare with the same type of work product.

KEY TAKE AWAY: All 3 reviews happened on the same project within a 15-day period on three separate large buckets of documents and with increasingly tight deadlines.

CLIENT REACTION: The client who has done many reviews asked us on the day we met the final deadline with complete candour, how we accomplished this seemingly impossible task?

Case study 13: 'Relief pitcher' project

In this project we were asked to replace an on-site review team in Minneapolis, which was reviewing about 15 documents an hour across a review team of 15 attorneys. I call it the Relief Pitcher project because in baseball, when pitchers get tired or in trouble during a game, a team will sometimes replace them with a new pitcher to avoid a disaster and to try to remain in the game in the hope that they can catch up. In this case, the disaster happened in the first week of the project.

The placement agency that supplied the review team was a national agency with offices in dozens of cities. They were highly respected, but they were off to such a slow start that the law firm realised the production deadline was going to be missed. The law firm, one of the hundred largest in the United States, said that if we could solve the problem, it would be a great opportunity to show how much better our remote review model was.

Within two days of the call, we had a top-quality review team assembled. The team averaged 42 documents per hour and finished before the deadline. Every reviewer on the team averaged more than 30 documents an hour, doubling the average of the original team of reviewers. This case was a class action with multiple defendants. If our client had not met the deadline and the other litigants did, we would have looked pretty bad. I had no problem motivating the team about how this project could show the world how much better remote review is. To continue the baseball metaphor, they delivered a homerun.

16. What is the right model for your project?

Every market has a different level of experience with document review, and as discussed at the beginning of this chapter, jurisdictions have different rules defining how much of a party's records must be disclosed to the other side. Based on my experience, there are four models that can be used. Each has its strengths and weaknesses. They are:

- law firms;
- technology companies;
- review companies; and
- corporate law departments.

There is no one right answer. Many participants can do good review work, but lots of them can easily do a poor job and not be caught. The outcome is unfortunately a part of the review space. It costs money to monitor – as well as to do – document review and to do it well is more than just putting some attorneys behind computer terminals. That, unfortunately, is the biggest barrier to improvement.

16.1 Other law firms

Law firms are a logical source of document review support. They understand the underlying need for the documents. They typically employ lots of lawyers who could be used to do the review.[59] If they do not have enough lawyers on their staff, they can contract for more lawyers at a lower billing rate and oversee the project. The problem is that law firms often bill at the highest rates for their services. Their departments often see different priorities for the firm's investments, and electronic discovery can be expensive and seem far from what lawyers typically do.

They understand the value of hiring the best review attorneys and treating them as an important part of doing electronic discovery work. Very few lawyers go to this level. They also have law firms that support them and have allowed them to make the investments necessary to do document review well.

16.2 Technology companies

Technology companies are another natural player in the document review space.[60] They are building or deploying the tools that make review faster, more accurate and less expensive. They understand how to do very good document review projects.

The downside to most technology companies doing document review is that they are better at managing technology and data than people. Review is powered by people. Most technology companies who hire reviewers to bid for projects are just looking for bodies to put alongside their technology. They are usually totally focused on how much the attorneys cost and the rates that they can bill for them.

In my experience, they tend not to put too much credence in the value of finding the best review attorneys. This is not to say they try to hire bad attorneys, just that metrics are not typically used to make their hiring decisions. In fact, many of them just hire a staffing company to do the recruiting for them. Usually being a step away from recruiting, they have little insight into how to improve the sourcing of who does their reviews.

Getting past a culture driven by technology tools and data management and into better human resources management can be a difficult path to adopt. However, if law firms do not embrace doing an excellent job in document review, there is not much market pressure for technology shops to do the same.

16.3 Review companies

Another group are review companies. In this group, there are a few staffing companies who still focus independently on document review.

"The downside to corporations tackling review in-house is that the politics and priorities of in-house legal departments can change whenever there are changes at the top of the law department, which can impact their ability and predisposition to perform document review in-house."

They have the advantage of recruiting and paying the reviewers. They have the potential of relating to the reviewers as an important part of their business model.

The problem is that seldom do these companies treat reviewers like serious professionals or the equals of the professional staff in technology companies or attorneys in law firms. In many cases, that treatment is justified.

To gain the confidence of clients, a staffing company has to be aware of the different technology tools being used in review and, importantly, how to get access to data from the review to create an intelligent rating system of the reviewers. This is not impossible to do, but in most cases, given the large number of underemployed lawyers, agencies tend to treat their review teams like anonymous bums on seats. This does not facilitate good review.

Having so many services supplying attorneys, but not on the basis of quality, also makes it harder to make a high enough margin to pay the best review attorneys the higher rate which they deserve compared to the rest of the field.[61] There are, however, a few companies advertising online that appear to be adopting the remote model. If they are doing it for quality reasons instead of cost reasons, they might be on the right path.

16.4 Corporate law departments

The last group consists of the corporate clients themselves. Document review is challenging but not impossible for serial litigants who are frequently having to evaluate records for litigation.[62] In addition to a much lower cost to do the review than hiring outside teams, an in-house team gets a certain familiarity with the documents used by an in-house client. The downside to corporations tackling review in-house is that the politics and priorities of in-house legal departments can change whenever there are changes at the top of the law department, which can impact their ability and predisposition to perform document review in-house.

17. Today's challenges

As more of the world begins to grapple with document review, there are several almost universal challenges that are highly relevant.

The first is how to make the new technology like predictive coding really save money for clients and create more accuracy with less training. Training software for a case requires finding enough documents that are part of the case and letting the software know it needs to find more of them.

How do you start the process? You need to find some documents to train the system. If you aim the system at what you know, you will likely find only more of what you already know. But what about what you don't know? A creative way to attack this is to develop fake documents based on the types of issues typically seen in antitrust cases, labour cases or other types of cases. Firms that specialise in a particular area of law should be able to develop 10 or more documents that can train a system to look for certain types of issues. This is an emerging area.

As second area is quality. Law firms should do more quality control work and use analytics to assess their reviewers. Any time many reviewers are put on a project, even the best technology will not work as designed because it will not be able to decipher what is good coding and what is bad coding. Some of the tools highlight inconsistent coding and kick those documents out for further review. By sampling and doing quality control work, the importance of quality is reinforced, especially with coders you do not know well, as well as ones who are coding too fast, too slowly, or making too many of the same types of coding mistakes.

Foreign language review has always been a bit of a black box for most people. How do you manage what you can't read? Some of the best review managers have reported that the worst coding they have ever seen was usually in foreign language reviews. The only testing done in this area is usually for language fluency, but there was not much done to determine who were actually very good reviewers in that foreign language. History demonstrates that reviewers whose native language is English or are fluent in English are not all great review attorneys. So why should fluency be the sole measure of being an effective reviewer? I would suggest developing the same methodology we developed for screening applicants for document review projects to recruit more foreign review attorneys. Because there are fewer of these attorneys, it is a field which appears well suited for remote review. With the extremely high cost of hiring foreign review attorneys, it makes sense to try to improve this area.

Finally, document review should be included in the curriculum of leading continuing professional education programmes in the field of electronic discovery. If it is assumed, as it widely is, that 70% of the costs of electronic discovery are in the review of documents, why is it impossible to have intelligent discussions on how to do review better? Why hasn't there been more research on the various approaches to document review? Better document review can save money and produce significant quality advantages in the final work product. It can make a tremendous difference for clients.

Acknowledgements
I sit in the pool area of my *pousada* looking at the most beautiful ocean view with volcanic remnants in the form of deserted islands and the waves hitting them. Birds are flying overhead in a nature scene that I now call home and my new business. I no longer wonder why the potential of outsourced document review is not explored more deeply, but I do know that it should be. With no plans to revisit the legal services industry at this time, this chapter is my parting gift to the profession and the many friends I made over the years.

I want to recognise some of the best review attorneys I have worked with in the past. They were all independent contractors when I interacted with them. Some of them have moved on to other companies or positions. To the extent being listed in a chapter about doing better document review can act as a reference, I wanted to do something nice for a group who frequently do not know where their next project will come from. This is a true all-star team, and I learned a lot from working closely with all of them. I may not have brought them to the promised land of perfect document review, but we did move the field forward with our experiences. I hope this chapter captures that idea and helps others to continue this journey.

So, thank you to: Robbie Robinson, Nick Cigrich, Linda Dunson, Marcia Luke, John Shrode, Leslie Sherman, Kim Yi, Mark McGhee, Anna Korolyvov, Neil Rubin, Jonathan Martz, Kelly Atherton, Gina Florez, Ed Walter, Bren Thissen, James Wheeler, Jarrold Turner, Brian Calla, Kathy Love Maxie, Andrea Cunningham, Michael Dinerman, Julienne Landsdown, Steven Ross, Rachel Stevens and Brian Harrison.

Notes

1 More importantly, I see this chapter as potentially saving lives which could be at risk doing document review work during a pandemic in review centres that, due to the need for air conditioning to control computer equipment, could unwittingly act as petri dishes for the virus.

2 As will be seen in this chapter, I have a strong preference for remote review but will cover all configurations of that service. Also, I am not selling any services with this chapter and have a non-compete agreement in effect until 17 January 2022, based on the sale of a review service for which I was co-CEO for most of my tenure. Due to the non-compete agreement, I may not disclose non-public information about my former company, such as details about the testing software for reviewers, for which I designed much of the functionality. However, there is plenty of useful public and other verifiable information that I will reference, based on my experience developing, managing and marketing review services.

3 *Global Aerospace Inc v Landow Aviation LP* (Loudon County, Va Cir Ct, 23 April 2012). Relevant memoranda and supporting documents are available at www.ediscoverylaw.com/files/2013/11/MemoSupportPredictiveCoding.pdf.

4 *In re: Garlock Sealing Technologies LLC*, US Dist Ct (WD, North Carolina), No 3:17-cv-00275-GCM (filed 12 June 2017). This was the only time I was able to act as the client in a review matter.

5 I eventually merged my company into a larger company where I became co-CEO. Two years later, our model had shown itself to be so successful that we were bought by a private equity company.

6 When I met with Brazilian lawyers in 2018 to discuss how to do document review better, their initial reaction was that their disclosure rules protect them from having to do reviews such as are done in the United States. So, your model for document review does not apply to our legal system, was their typical first response.

7 My company prepared a proposal for the Volkswagen investigation, and while not successful, we were contracted for corollary review in Germany with another automotive-related company.

8 The Brazilian law firms that I examined in 2018 were not large. While there are a handful of large (400+ attorneys) law firms, many of the successful litigation practices are in smaller firms in the

20–75 attorney range. In my opinion, many of them look like law firms in the United States before electronic data became widespread and document review took off. At that point in time, in order for law firms to convince clients they could handle larger electronic data reviews, they had to grow in size. This is a prevailing profile of most law firms in most of the jurisdictions worldwide, ie of a size and with limited internal resources that would make a typically large document-review function very difficult, if not impossible, for them to perform entirely in-house.

9 I visited a large pharmaceutical company in 2003 and explained why they were paying much more for the review than necessary by also having large second-pass reviews. Incredibly, the lawyer who managed this department and its budgets said, "Is it really a big problem if we think we are saving money?" This was also at a time when big law firms would provide their clients with a single-page monthly bill with no backup explanations about the "professional services rendered". Ten years later, in 2013, I presented a show on my podcast series ESIBytes with David Howard, the head of litigation at Microsoft, where he described in detail how much it cost for Microsoft to manage all the electronic records in a litigation. These costs included collections, data holds and, eventually, review. They had offered a critique about the need to reduce these costs in the form of a letter to the relevant committee in the US government then considering amendments to the Federal Rules of Civil Procedure. While not specifically a component of improving document review, cost is a huge part of its history.

10 Interestingly, this firm had hired me for a summer position in 1991 but did not offer me a job. I was crushed at the time. When I got this project in 1999, the partner who had not hired me told me that I was just like a partner in a law firm now, looking for a temporary lawyer to do work that I would have done as an associate.

11 It also put my company on the map as one of the fastest-growing companies in the United States.

12 Our company, Legal Network, had just appeared on the Inc. 500 list ranking the fastest-growing companies in the United States, and we were ranked as the second-fastest growing company in our home city of Pittsburgh, Pennsylvania. As an MBA-trained lawyer, I had always focused my selling of this service on the profitability of review done with outsourced review attorneys. My partner, Olga Schieneman, and I built a piece of software called StaffRite, with the help of Norman Clark, the editor of this book, who was a principal of Altman Weil Inc, and, later in its development, the founding principal of the international legal management consultancy of Walker Clark LLC. StaffRite also used national law firm cost data collected by Altman Weil Inc, in its annual *Survey of Law Firm Economics*. Using actual law firm operating costs and overheads, StaffRite built project cost-estimating models empirically proving the economic advantage of doing outsourced document review instead of using in-house law firm associates. StaffRite and our success with this second large project enabled us to develop a dominant position in our Pittsburgh market, and we staffed 22 of the 25 largest law firms in the city.

13 I believed that the law firm was trying to get me to threaten to pull the review team off the project until we got paid, but we got paid immediately. However, this gave the law firm a reason to bring in three other external staffing agencies to staff the same project we had helped to bid with them. Soon after, attorneys from four different agencies were working side-by-side with our very large review team. We were given 70% of the review work, but the other agencies were guaranteed a certain percentage as well. The result worked as far as the law firm and client was concerned but it created a human resources problem that consumed almost all of my time on the project for the next 18 months. I had to speak personally for the first time with many of my 170 employees and deal with the other agencies trying to offer better benefits or higher wages to try to recruit away my team. With hindsight, this was invaluable as I learned much more about who the attorneys were and all of their concerns. It also taught me a lot about the review business that I had not touched, and which a financial model like StaffRite could not teach me. These insights framed many of the strategies I adopted in the second half of my career to improve document review.

14 Another good example of how document reviewers can feel is the anger and mistrust I encountered the week we sold Legal Network in August 2004. No one knew when the project, discussed in case study 2, was going to end, and the buyer did not want to pay millions of dollars for a project which could end at any point and had already wound down to less than half its largest size. So, they elected not to buy this project. They bought everything else and agreed to let me support the project to try and get more projects from these clients. I then had to tell the remaining 80 contract attorneys that they were still working on the project and were not part of the sale. They now worked for a ghost company with no other clients. They were not happy. We were able to negotiate a new deal which included a form of health insurance, and a pay increase for the team. My team was now going to be paid more than any other reviewers in the local market and were very happy. Everyone ended ahead.

15 A QCer was an attorney who would review samples of documents to make sure the first review was accurate. Who was right: the QCer or the attorney who did the first review? I remember these discussions vividly.

16 The team leaders on my projects were usually all employed by Legal Network, as were the managers, some of whom had been hired away by the law firm. I had a great relationship with all of them. As a result, I had frequent meetings with these managers to learn what challenges they faced to achieve a good production result from the review. From this I recognised that improving the review's working environment and the treatment of the team could pay dividends to a project.

17 In one instance, one of the fastest document review attorneys with whom I have ever worked was removed from a project because the client did not believe the metrics on her résumé. I investigated this and was able to get her back on the team, but it took a lot of convincing. In my experience, there

are some reviewers who have incredible speed and accuracy. We had one attorney who was a critical force when we wanted to push hard to speed up a review. Everyone on the team knew that this individual would plough through documents at a fast speed. We had another attorney who was not only fast, but could work extremely accurately in the nuanced world of privileged documents. I often had her working directly with partners at some of the biggest law firms in the country. Everyone who has worked on document reviews knows there are some stars and lots of mediocre and poor reviewers. Most reviews include some form of quality control work or second-pass reviews, and the people who perform those functions have usually been promoted to their position because they are the best first-pass reviewers.

18 I was proud of the structure we had helped to put together, and proud of the team. I know the client was proud too because they made many presentations on how they refused to settle the cases but would only settle based on legitimate claims as opposed to grouping all claims that a particular lawyer was bringing together and settling all of them. This strategy was based on lowering the discovery costs by using temporary lawyers.

19 I did not personally participate in this document review. This case study is based on information provided to me by attorneys who participated in the project, whom I know to be reliable sources.

20 For example, I produced 25 podcasts, as part of my free series *ESIBytes*, which included judges and practitioners trying to bring more technology into the legal field generally to solve problems facing lawyers in electronic discovery such as how to use predictive coding.

21 I met with judges and explained the opportunities to perform faster, more accurate reviews. At the time, many judges were unsure if there was anything they could do. Litigants have the right to pick their own tools. The message to the judges was simple: Do not tell litigants who to do the reviews; just let them know it is okay to use more technology. The judges with whom I met became cheerleaders for the new technology at a time when almost no one was using technology to assist with document reviews.

22 Seeing the growing momentum for predictive coding by 2011, and the absence of skilled practitioners to implement it in the legal profession, I formed my own company called Review Less to focus on the intersection between using technology and the possibilities of doing document review better with better-skilled review attorneys working on smaller review teams. I decided to use the same data to build a test of a document reviewer's accuracy, which could be used for hiring, training and quality assurance. I was not sure how to fit document review into the world of predictive coding, but I knew enough to understand that the predictive coding needed a base of good reviewers who could train the software about what types of documents to look for in any collection. Moreover, although there might have been a few hundred influential people in the predictive coding space at that time, there were no more than a handful of people who were even thinking about using it to do better document review. I started using our software test in about eight cities and recruited about 1,000 attorneys using the test results for correct coding and speed to determine which candidates I would interview.

23 One amazing project that I did borrowed some technology which does not exist anymore in commercial use, that a lawyer friend was using at the time. Meta data is very important to any computer-assisted review. It is like fingerprints or DNA are to a detective investigating a case. Meta data is the unique data about a document that is stored on a computer. Examples of meta data are the creation date, author of a document, people who received a document, whether the document was read, how many times it was read, when it was read, and the key words in the document. By leveraging meta data, this powerful software presented a visible timeline which showed the people and the types of documents involved, as well as central themes from the documents. Over three days, we used this tool and a small team of reviewers on a population of 375,000 documents, analysing eight issues. Using traditional review tools to do the same review in three days would have taken more than 260 attorneys. The total cost was $150,000 which was $0.39 per document at a time when clients typically considered $1.25 per document to be cost-effective.

24 *Global Aerospace Inc v Landow Aviation LP* (Loudon County, Va Cir Ct, 23 April 2012).

25 I saw similar results personally and among review attorneys using a document review test I created. The recall scores were consistently in the 70% range when applied to the same Enron document set used in the TREC studies and in four of the document categories TREC used. Several large law firms contested these results as being lower than what they identified in their reviews, but they never provided any data to rebut these findings.

26 Ironically, the firm that challenged our use of this software was also the firm which did not like the software we had used in the earlier case. Several years after this result, after multiple meetings with this firm, their litigation department became a big fan of predictive coding.

27 *In re: Garlock Sealing Technologies LLC*, US Dist Ct (WD, North Carolina), No 3:17-cv-00275-GCM (filed 12 June 2017). For a narrative account of the case, see "In re: Garlock Sealing Technologies, LLC", Wikipedia, https://en.wikipedia.org/wiki/In_re_Garlock_Sealing_Technologies%2C_LLC.

28 One problem was that this technology had never been used in a large case before, let alone a billion-dollar case with work that could find its way up to the US Supreme Court for a final review to determine whether our analysis could be used in thousands of other asbestos litigation cases across the United States. Another challenge was that the new technology required licensing of the software and we had bought only four licences. To keep all four licences working, our software to select the best review attorneys was vital. We put 11 attorneys on the project in three different regions working eight-hour shifts and then handing on the licence to the next person on the project. My client was the bankruptcy court which approved our creative solution to a very messy problem. The party paying the bills was a lawyer who had no idea what we were trying to do at first, but felt lots of pressure to

decide – before approving our bills – whether this was a good decision. I presented a large budget, which assigned 75 review attorneys to the project, and a much more modest budget using our new technology solution. I got him to agree to let us try using the technology on the first asbestos trust with two attorneys and see if it worked. After less than a week, we could see it was working. We got approval to move ahead and staffed the project with 11 attorneys and one team leader.

29 I also designed a training course for lawyers to help them use this new technology, which was presented in 10 cities and included panels of local judges and local lawyers, as well as audio clips from nationally famous judges. We walked lawyers through the mathematics so they would be comfortable with the results of predictive coding, even if they did not understand how the technology worked.

30 The project described in the third of the three case studies immediately above was our first real test of a remote review team working 18 hours across multiple time zones. The management of a remote review is very time-intensive and requires managers to work much harder. Thus, it is critical that the reviewers be good reviewers. I was lucky – I had a great team. My skill-testing software predicted that they would be great. My team also knew that I had put my faith, and to some extent my career reputation, on the line because I believed in them. I told them they were the best reviewers in the country. As a result, they worked so hard that in the last week when I had to leave the country for family reasons, and when my team leader's car got hit by a drunk driver as he was leaving the hospital visiting a dying parent, my next two best reviewers stepped into his shoes so that the project did not suffer.

31 Not actually owning any predictive coding tools, I decided at that time to turn all of my attention back to document review. Everyone needed to do review, but not everyone needed or wanted to use predictive coding. After doing an educational tour around the country, I felt that while it would not be impossible to teach lawyers how to use statistics to get comfortable with predictive coding, it would be difficult to get them comfortable with the idea that predictive coding was not going to eliminate many lawyer jobs. So, I decided to focus all I had learned to produce the best document reviews possible. If clients wanted to use predictive coding, that was great too, but we were going to leave that decision up to the clients.

32 Having owned a legal staffing agency in Pittsburgh, a metropolitan area of 2.3 million inhabitants, for five years, I understood very well how difficult it could be to staff, with high-quality people, a review project in a single city if there was a major case already going on in the same market.

33 I made this exact point when debating with a large law firm during a CLE programme in Pittsburgh in 2017. The firm's attorney said they could identify a banking expert, a nurse review attorney and an engineer attorney to put on any project. My response was with a national pool of 10,000 tested lawyers to draw from, I could find 20–30 of them in one day, while the law firm had a pool of only 50–60 specialised attorneys available.

34 This was the entire premise for selling Pittsburgh as the review site during the litigation described in case study 2. Pittsburgh lawyers at the time cost about $8 an hour less than document review lawyers in New York or Washington.

35 This might be complicated in the United States, where lawyers are licensed by each state, not nationally. In some states, it can be difficult for an out-of-state lawyer to open a new law practice in a new location without passing that state's bar examination. However, some states permit contracted document review work to be performed if a lawyer is licensed to practise law in any US state or territory.

36 There were many projects I can recall where there were elaborate plans to pay attorneys who were not working or to create other things to do just to not lose the review team in case the review project heated back up again. Once it was disassembled, an on-site review team was likely going to move to other projects around the city. Remote review does not have this problem. Because most projects last only a few weeks, losing attorneys to a short-term project during a lull in your project is not the worst outcome for anyone, especially the attorneys who need to make money.

37 Today I have the first eco hotel certified for sustainability in Brazil, which makes this issue especially important to me. Early on at Review Less, one of my companies, I calculated the eco savings from doing remote review and was astounded at how much energy is saved. It is hard to get precise numbers on the environmental cost savings from doing remote review. However, using common sense and general statistics found from searching the internet, it is easy to see that the cost savings can be substantial.

38 Buildings and their construction together account for 36% of global energy use and 39% of energy-related carbon dioxide emissions annually, according to the United Nations Environment Program. See, eg, Diana Budds, "How Do Buildings Contribute to Climate Change" (*Curbed*, 19 September 2019), https://archive.curbed.com/2019/9/19/20874234/buildings-carbon-emissions-climate-change. It was estimated in 2018 that 20% of all energy costs are for air conditioning in buildings.

39 One year at Special Counsel, we had a 30-person review that the general counsel of the client was suggesting he would move from the outside law firm to us if a production date was not met. We brought in dinners, did dry cleaning and worked seven days a week for several weeks. Ultimately, we hit the deadline, working in our review centre in a building in downtown Pittsburgh of which we were one tenant in a 30-storey building. Several months after that push, I received a bill for $5,000 from the office building, which was the cost to keep this building air conditioned. Based on a hidden provision in our lease, we paid for the air conditioning of the entire building over the weekends that month. Normally, the building would have turned off the air conditioning on weekends, but in midsummer, we absolutely need it. It was too late to bill the client for this additional expense, as the

project was over. So, I brought a plastic bag with some ice cubes in it and took my client to lunch and gave it to him as my gift.
40 http://blueskymodel.org/gallon-gas.
41 If we are going to ever rein in the use of fossil fuels and carbon dioxide emissions, we are going to have to look at every opportunity to reduce global emissions. This was a tough argument to make in the United States when I started doing remote review. The Paris Climate Agreement, signed by 195 countries around the world, would reduce emissions from rising more than 2°C by curbing the amount of greenhouse gas emissions allowed by each participating nation. Switching document review to remote review as a standard review model is one way the legal community can offer a strategy to participate in helping combat global warming.
42 When I merged my home-based review company, Review Less, into the more traditional review company called Inspired Review, we issued a press release where I touted the 48 straight successful projects in a row we had staffed before the merger – a 48-0 record, almost on par with Rocky Marciano, the heavyweight boxing champion of the world who won 49 straight fights and retired before he lost one. We always came in under budget with quality results that thrilled clients. That perfect record continued after merging into Inspired Review. In fact, I never staffed a single on-site review after I sold Legal Network in 2004 and left Special Counsel in 2007. I was proud of this record. But, most importantly, it is the most humane model for document reviewers.
43 The interview was a critical time for me or a recruiter to tell a top review attorney how working for my service would be different from a local review service that might give most of the work to that particular attorney. I could never compete with such an agency, but I could work with such candidates when they had time and give them a great experience working with other excellent document review attorneys. I made the point, "Not everyone can work for us. You did great on the test". I did feel bad for attorneys who did not do well on the test and would email us to complain. I understood their concern and frustration. However, the job of anyone recruiting a review team is to filter whom to pick. I found testing useful and something that could be incorporated into document review recruiting software.
44 I have often been asked questions like: *How do you train the team?*; *How do you conduct your meetings to discuss what you are seeing?*; and *How do you know your team is working and not goofing off?* A chat room, to which the entire team has access, answers most of these questions and demonstrates to outside counsel that there is a talented review team at work. Outside counsel can see from the questions raised during training and during the review that the review team is taking its responsibility seriously.
45 Most reviewers I knew well said they had never seen such a culture before. This is not something we instilled in them. All we did is give them the tools and told them they were good. Their professionalism and desire to do a good job did the rest and built the culture. It happened time and time again.
46 Truthfully, we occasionally had issues with friendly banter as in any office setting. We would just remind the team that the client can and would likely see the chat. So, please keep it professional and 95% work-related.
47 When I first instituted chat, I remembered that I had worked with a project management tool called Basecamp when I created the virtual law firm I launched in 2007. If lower income individuals, who were most of my clients, with little software or internet skills could access and use these tools with little training, I thought a law firm partner who did not feel comfortable with technology could do the same.
48 For example, WhatsApp, a secure communication tool, which an estimated 70% of all Brazilians use and which is widely used for secure communications among lawyers worldwide, could be configured as group chat among the review team and easily opened on a dual monitor system while doing a review.
49 I would not say that we had 100% all-star reviewers on most projects I staffed. Some reviewers would disappear temporarily if they were busy on another on-site project. However, with 70% highly skilled review attorneys, the poor habits of a few could be offset while still hitting production deadlines under budget and with high quality. Even without having total control over who was working on a project at any given point of the day or evening, having a high percentage of high-quality reviewers really created a huge advantage. Attorneys who disappeared could be considered poor performers and usually would not be used again.
50 On reviews where we had 70% outstanding review attorneys, our quality control attorneys could get by with sampling the first review set. We would also focus our total quality control effort on batches for attorneys with whom we had never worked before. Having an experienced review team of all-star reviewers makes it easier for the managers to help with quality control.
51 I usually budgeted less for quality checks in order to get a price advantage, but I would ask to pay review attorneys a bit more than usual for the first-pass review. This was often hard to accomplish, and review rates have been dropping even for the best review attorneys. This is unfortunate because, at the end of the day, I did not see clients saving money by investing lots of review time into quality control when we had done the review so well in the first instance. Moreover, I could not ethically charge our clients for more quality control searches if they were not necessary.
52 See case study 2.
53 This is something rarely done in the document review industry. I did it on every occasion I had to. The regulatory agency and the law firm became very good clients going forward.
54 After developing the remote review model and seeing it work time after time, I was proud of our team and the results. Because of the chat tools, many of the team knew each other and respected

the work product of their teammates. This was something rare in the industry. After merging with the new company, we had to show that it worked. For the first year it felt like two different companies going in different directions. Eventually I had to have the chief operating officer terminated when text messages showed he was rooting against our remote review at times and picking friends of his to get on review projects instead of using the data. In fact, his friends were refusing to sign up for the software and to be tested and would not return phone calls I made to them. This reaction is not unusual because of how review projects are often staffed.

55 By using data and the front end of the software I designed, I was able, on occasions, to recruit my own projects single-handedly, including a 100-attorney project both on-site and off-site with a large law firm that wanted to see the difference between the review teams we could offer. I personally recruited the project and sent two teams to them in 48 hours. They were amazed, and they could also clearly see that the quality of the remote review team was much higher than the on-site review team. This was the result that I wanted to see, not only to win this work but for future marketing purposes.

56 I believe strongly that this type of work, due to its limited duration in many situations, could avoid creating employment relationships. I won three times with this argument (in Texas, Illinois and Germany) and my one loss was in New York state. Shortly after we lost in New York, we stopped working remotely with all attorneys there, and it did not cause us any other issues. Germany was much more favourable and even issued an opinion. In that matter an attorney, seeking to benefit from the strong labour laws in Germany, resigned from the project after one hour of training. Then, in the following year, he sued for one month's salary and for legal fees as allowed under German labour law. Apparently, he had done this two times before and had been paid by other agencies. I refused to settle and we hired a German law firm. Our argument was simple: How can I guarantee someone a month's salary when the project might end in a week? Plumbers or outside law firms are not paid a month's salary for every project. The court agreed and the case against us was dismissed.

57 A colleague of mine used to say that large monitors or dual monitors added 15–20% more speed to the document review. I have not seen a study confirming this, but common sense says the reviews are much faster with dual monitors.

58 See case study 5.

59 I can suggest two examples of lawyers who, in my experience, know how to do review correctly. The first is Dave Cohen. Dave is a Harvard lawyer who decided to focus his career away from litigation towards electronic discovery. What he has done exceptionally well in document review is offering his review team a stable salary in return for lower billable hour requirements than required from his associates. He treats them and markets them like the best in the industry. He has moved them beyond document review tasks and utilises their legal skills. This of course makes the review attorneys feel more appreciated than most in the industry. He utilises Pittsburgh as a low-cost region to have a document review team based. All of this has combined to help keep them busy for many years on numerous projects. After the outbreak of the COVID-19 pandemic, he moved to, and likes, remote review.

A different model is deployed by Bennett Borden. Bennett is the first data scientist lawyer, having created an education path to get academic credentials as a data scientist. Bennett was also the first lawyer I know actively doing remote document review. While Bennett, like Dave Cohen, does not touch the document review work, he had built a team that is agile and talented. They can typically leverage advanced technology and use analytics and statistics to supplement any review strategy they deploy.

The work of both Dave and Bennett are great examples of lawyers who can do document review and excel at it. But both do not dabble in this field. They are experts across the technology.

60 When I was developing ReviewRight, we worked with several technology companies. Eventually we were acquired by one. They continue to deploy what we built and have the tools to do document review very effectively. Some of my trusted advisers who managed my reviews have joined other technology or review companies.

61 As I have described throughout this chapter, my experience demonstrates that independent review companies can be built to provide superior document review services, but it is not easy.

62 In 2017, I showed the front end of testing software I had designed to one of the largest technology companies on the planet. We were further along than the work this wealthy company had done in-house to manage litigation. Therefore, they did not need our professional services, but they were in complete support of our vision. Because their focus was to have metrics showing the effort of their review task to convince judges that the reviews were disproportionately expensive compared to the actual litigation, I imagine they were also evaluating the performance of this small team of less than 20 review attorneys.

V. The future of outsourcing in the legal services industry

Norman K Clark
Fernando Moreno
Walker Clark LLC[1]

1. A thought experiment for 2025

It is 2025. You have done an admirable job of managing your law firm through the 'COVID Recession of 2020–2021', but, as in previous recessions, you have not quite returned to 'normalcy'. As you expected, competition has increased, especially from non-traditional competitors, and is more intense than ever before. During the downturn, both old and new clients became more price-sensitive, including for services that you had always considered to be 'premium' or 'high value'. Everyone now demands big discounts – whether for 'client loyalty' or 'volume' or as a 'new client' promotion. It sometimes seems that your competitors, even the old well-established ones, are now willing to do legal work almost for free and sometimes, you suspect, even at a loss simply to hold onto current clients and lure new ones from other firms, including yours. This is a trend that shows no signs of reversing.

At the same time, after two years of operating costs being somewhat reduced due to pandemic-related reductions in areas such as facilities expenses, travel costs and marketing, these and other operating costs are beginning to go back almost to – or in some instances above – pre-pandemic levels. The biggest pressure is in personnel costs, which has always consumed the largest portion of your firm's operating costs. Associates, paralegals and experienced support staff are expecting salary increases, motivated in part by a general feeling that they deserve them in return for staying with the firm during the pandemic and the recession, enduring pay cuts that were temporary but never fully recovered, and working remotely often at the cost of significant interference to their family needs and priorities during the public health crisis. Now that the 'good times' appear to be returning, at least according to the news media and politicians, some of your best colleagues are seriously considering high-paying opportunities elsewhere.

In short, your firm's profitability is being squeezed by lower revenue and higher costs, and every indicator suggests that, if you continue business as usual, that pressure will become even more intense in the coming years. Your firm's business manager and several of your partners say that your firm needs to 'rethink' its basic operating structures, the way that it prepares and delivers services to clients. "We have to jettison some of the dead weight", says your business manager, who is an avid sailor. "We need to think about outsourcing."

What will you do and how will you do it?

2. Law firms as assembly plants

The authors maintain, based on their experience and observations in the legal market today, that this thought experiment, even if conducted today, could result in a complete outsourcing of almost all of the core legal functions of a traditional law firm. We are not advocating such an approach as a universal 'best practice' or goal; instead, we merely point out that it would be possible today. By 2025, when our thought experiment is set, it could be a survival imperative for many law firms, especially small and mid-sized firms.

The past 30 years have seen profound changes in the mission, structure and operations of law firms worldwide. The most obvious transformations, some of them almost revolutionary in nature, have been in the size, geographic dispersal and multidisciplinary nature of the services that law firms deliver. Legal process outsourcing is not a recent development, however. Some commonly outsourced functions, such as accounting, recruiting, 'surge staffing' by contracted attorneys, document review and patent research, have been available since the late 1990s. What is new today, however, is that rather than contracting external service providers to provide these services and products on a matter-by-matter basis, there now exists the opportunity to outsource these and other functions entirely and permanently.

In almost every country and jurisdiction in the world, it is possible today to outsource virtually every internal operating function, including the work that lawyers do, to an outside service provider that,

"The past 30 years have seen profound changes in the mission, structure and operations of law firms worldwide. The most obvious transformations, some of them almost revolutionary in nature, have been in the size, geographic dispersal and multidisciplinary nature of the services that law firms deliver."

in most instances, can do the same work at the same or better levels of professional quality and at a lower cost than retaining that work in-house. The fast, secure worldwide delivery of sophisticated products and services via the internet has made this possible even in the smallest commercial centres and most remote parts of the globe.

What this means is that between 2021 and 2030, we can expect many law firms to restructure their core legal service functions in ways that will change the basic model of the law firm from a professional services factory to that of an assembly plant.

Under the traditional 'factory' model, a law firm produced its products and services entirely in-house, with little or no direct support from, or involvement by, outsiders. The few functions that were contracted from external vendors usually involved purely administrative, logistical or financial support functions – the 'back room' operations. Outsourcing was particularly attractive for small law firms, most of which simply did not have the staff or resources to perform these tasks in-house.

Under the 'assembly plant' model, much of the underlying preparation, research and expert analysis required to prepare a legal service for delivery to the client is provided by outsiders who can deliver the same

"Indeed, looking forward to 2030 and the years beyond, the authors expect to see the emergence of completely virtual global law firms that deliver legal products and services to clients anywhere in the world at a fraction of the fee that traditional 'bricks and mortar' law firms currently charge and at greater profitability."

quality of research, knowledge and analytical insight as the law firm could do internally, but at a substantially lower cost and usually with more consistent high levels of professional and service-delivery quality. Like an aircraft assembly plant, these law firms take the components they contract from external suppliers and apply their own legal expertise, experience and intimate knowledge of the client's objectives and expectations to design and 'assemble' a highly-customised service and solution.

We believe that, over the next 10 years, the economic and competitive survival of traditional law firms will be determined in part by their ability to make well-informed, commercially-aware decisions about how, and to what extent, they must convert from the old factory model, which for most of them – and especially for small and mid-size law firms – will no longer be financially sustainable, to a well-designed and well-executed assembly plant model. Indeed, looking forward to 2030 and the years beyond, the authors expect to see the emergence of completely virtual global law firms that deliver legal products and services to clients anywhere in the world at a fraction of the fee that traditional 'bricks and mortar' law firms currently charge and at greater profitability. Even if a completely virtual operational and service delivery structure is not right for a particular law firm, the challenge for each firm will be to determine which services it should outsource and which ones it should keep in-house. The absence of external providers of those services will not be a consideration.

3. Moving beyond profit and risk: conditions of success

The profitability-oriented evaluation that we recommend – ie, Where can we obtain the best long-term return on an investment in outsourcing? – and its risk-management overlay – ie, What risks, especially quality-related ones, are we willing to accept and be capable of managing? – are only the first steps. To be fully successful, and to avoid a costly crisis in service-delivery, quality, or information security, the owners of a law firm, whether a single proprietor or an entire partnership, should think through several basic issues, usually embedded deep in the firm's existing management practices and professional culture, that even the best outsourcing opportunity cannot solve. These include:

- **Are there flaws in our existing policies and procedures for the selection of external suppliers?** This involves more than a careful comparison of proposals and due diligence about the prospective supplier. It also involves the extent to which a law firm habitually selects external vendors without fully understanding the services, functions or tasks that it seeks to outsource. A bad selection usually starts with a weak, vague, or in some cases, delusional selection process.

- **Do we have performance measurements in place that can alert us to any emerging issues in the delivery of the outsourced functions and services?** Because these are usually very specific to the firm, to the services it delivers to clients, and to the internal management of its practice groups and service lines, do not expect an external supplier to supply these metrics 'off the shelf.'
- **Are our marketing and business development communications already focused on the delivery of differentiating benefits to clients?** Just asserting that you are supported by the best outside experts in the world is not enough. Has your firm sufficiently thought through your relationships with your clients and their most important needs and expectations, so that you can demonstrate – not just assert – how outsourcing gives your firm a superior advantage over your competitors? In other words, have you already moved beyond mere slogans? If you cannot do this with key services and service-delivery characteristics that you perform in-house, do not expect this to improve suddenly once you outsource one of the relevant core functions.
- **Do the leaders of your firm already know how to lead change?** The authors' colleague, Lisa M Walker Johnson, who is well-recognised as an international authority on change management in law firms, has pointed out that there are six essential components to leading and managing the major changes in law firms. We believe that they constitute a useful high-level checklist for a traditional law firm that wants to outsource a core legal function:
  - committed leadership;
  - data and evidence;
  - a compelling business case with financial markers;
  - a well-informed process;
  - other actions and solutions that fit the unique characteristics of the firm; and
  - shared measurable results.[2]

To what extent does your law firm already have these components built into the way that you lead change in the organisation? Moreover, how well does your firm respond to the three forces which can thwart even the best thought-out change process – conflict, chaos and inertia? As Ms Walker Johnson explains, these three process conditions:

> *... can derail any change effort very quickly, regardless of the partners' intent, preparation, or sense of urgency. At the same time, they are also natural, unavoidable and important conditions for change. Conflict, chaos and inertia also can be a tremendous force*

"How well does your firm respond to the three forces which can thwart even the best thought-out change process – conflict, chaos and inertia?"

> *for good by improving focus and motivation, problem solving, decision making and the implementation of strategic priorities.*
>
> *... [E]ach of these three conditions is a natural element of any planned change. If partners avoid or deny their existence and therefore do not manage them well, positive planned change will not occur.*[3]

- **Does your firm understand how traditional paradigms in the practice of law might be holding you back from moving to a better future?** Two of the biggest challenges for traditional law firms are to break down the paradigms that prevent them from seeing the future – as well as fundamentally changed realities today – and to stimulate genuinely innovative responses.

Why is it that lawyers and law firms are so often surprised by disruptions in their own profession? Why do so many law firms always seem to be playing 'catch up' with their clients and the business world in general? Undoubtedly one of the biggest obstacles to law firms' ability to respond to change is the effect of the paradigms that have governed the way that they conceptualise and understand the practice of law. The word paradigm originates from the Greek *παράδειγμα*, which means example, model or pattern. Paradigms are mental assumptions that we make, based on our experiences in the world, that shape the way that we perceive certain situations and govern our actions in response to them. A paradigm can even cause us to fail to perceive things that we otherwise see. Traditional law firms with conservative, inward-looking professional cultures usually have the greatest difficulty, and experience the deepest disappointments in moving to greater outsourcing of core legal functions, because of the paradigm shifts that these steps frequently imply.

Even to perceive the future of the legal profession, much less actually to understand it, lawyers and law firms, as a matter of survival, must be willing to escape many of the paradigms that have shaped the practice of law for centuries, and which can prevent them from seeing new realities. As futurist Joel Barker[4] has said: "The role of leadership is to find, recognise, and secure the future".

Notes

1 Walker Clark LLC is an international legal management consultancy, based in the United States with team members also in Europe and Latin America. Founded in 2002, the firm's practice specialises in strategic, operational and performance advice and support to law firms, corporate and government legal departments, and professional services networks worldwide.
2 Lisa M Walker Johnson, "Managing Change" in Norman Clark, ed., *Good Governance in Law Firms: A Strategic Approach to Executive Decision Making and Management Structures* (London: Globe Law and Business, 2014), pp212–218
3 *Ibid*, pp218–219.
4 Joel Barker was the first person to popularise the concept of paradigm shifts in the corporate world. He began his work in 1975 after spending a year on fellowship meeting and working with visionary thinkers in both North America and Europe. He discovered that the concept of paradigms, which at that time was sequestered within the scientific discussion, could explain the revolutionary change in all areas of human endeavour. For more information, see www.joelbarker.com.

About the authors

Norman K Clark
Principal, Walker Clark LLC
norman.clark@walkerclark.com

Norman Clark is principal at Walker Clark LLC. His professional background is as a lawyer. Since 1996, he has worked exclusively as a consultant to law firms, corporate and government legal departments. His consulting practice focuses on issues of international business and legal practice strategy, mergers, quality assurance and risk management, internal productivity, partnership governance and remuneration, and lawyer performance, and profitability. He is also one of the world's leading authorities on business and marketing strategy for law firms in emerging markets, working with progressive law firms in Africa, Asia, the Caribbean, central and eastern Europe, Latin America and the Middle East.

Sitima Fowler
Co-founder and partner, Iconic IT
sfowler@iconicit.com

Sitima Fowler is co-founder and partner of Iconic IT, an award-winning managed IT service provider providing small and medium-sized organisations with local and responsive IT support services including fully managed or co-managed IT support, cybersecurity and cloud solutions. She has more than 20 years of industry experience in the field of technology, cybersecurity and business consulting.

Prior to her current role, Sitima was the co-CEO of Capstone IT, one of four companies that merged in 2019 to form Iconic IT. Her passion has been securing and improving small and medium-sized organisations with proper technology solutions, with an emphasis on customer service. She is an author and a professional speaker on a wide variety of topics including cybersecurity, sales and marketing and business strategies. The recipient of the Rochester, New York, USA's 2015 Small Businessperson of the Year and inventor of six patents, Sitima is also the founder of the #GetCyberChic initiative, whose goal is to inform female business leaders about online safety.

Tushar Gupta
Co-founder, Intricate Research
tushar.gupta@intricateresearch.com

Tushar Gupta is co-founder of Intricate Research, a Patent Research and Analytics firm which provides end-to-end patent solutions. He has more than 10 years of enriched experience in the field of telecom, patent research & analytics, and business research.

Prior to starting his own venture, he held leadership positions with a couple of multinational companies. Over the years, he has managed numerous clients spread across geographies and provided tailored business and patent solutions. He has developed business/operation processes and has played significant roles in building teams. He started his career with a global leader in telecom technologies. With an objective to bring IP awareness and foster IP culture, he has delivered a number of IP workshops relating to the importance of IP protection to academic institutes and start-ups.

Gaurav Khandelwal
Co-founder, Intricate Research
gaurav.k@intricateresearch.com

Gaurav Khandelwal is co-founder of Intricate Research, a Patent Research and Analytics firm which provides end-to-end patent solutions. He has more than 10 years of enriched experience in the field of patent research and analytics.

He has acquired hands-on industry experience in diverse patent-related services. In addition to a strong technical background, Gaurav has in-depth knowledge in US, EU and Indian patent prosecution laws. He has a client-centric approach which has helped him deliver solutions to his clients' delight.

Fernando Moreno
Principal, Walker Clark LLC
fernando.moreno@walkerclark.com

Fernando Moreno is a principal at Walker Clark LLC, with more than 20 years' experience in management and marketing consultancy for professional services firms and corporate legal departments worldwide. His practice concentrates on strategic planning, the development and implementation of marketing plans, feasibility studies for mergers and new products and ventures, law firm valuations, law firm economics, and general management coaching.

Karl Schieneman
Owner, Baia do Joao Eco Pousada
karlshin60501@gmail.com

Karl Schieneman is an entrepreneur lawyer who has worked in and owned several e-discovery companies, all of which have been successfully sold. He worked on the first computer-assisted review project in the United States (*Global Aerospace* case), was the first court-appointed Special Master in the US Bankruptcy Court overseeing a software driven review (*Garlock Asbestos* bankruptcy case), created the first online recruiting and review testing software (ReviewRight), co-developed with Norman Clark an economic model turned into software calculating law firm profitability by using interim staffing (StaffRite), and most recently sold his last e-discovery business and started the first certified sustainable Pousada in Buzios, Brazil called Baia do Joao Eco Pousada. A past winner of the Ernst & Young Entrepreneur of the Year Award in 2004, he has owned businesses involving legal services which have been on the Inc 500 List 12 times as one of the fastest growing companies in the United States. He earned an MBA from Carnegie Mellon University and a JD from the University of Pittsburgh, School of Law in 1992.

About Globe Law and Business

Globe Law and Business was established in 2005. From the very beginning, we set out to create law books which are sufficiently high level to be of real use to the experienced professional, yet still accessible and easy to navigate. Most of our authors are drawn from Magic Circle and other top commercial firms, both in the United Kingdom and internationally.

Our titles are carefully produced, with the utmost attention paid to editorial, design and production processes. We hope this results in high-quality books which are easy to read, and a pleasure to own. All our new books are also available as ebooks, which are compatible with most desktop, laptop and tablet devices. We have recently expanded our portfolio to include a new range of journals and Special Reports, available both digitally and in hard copy format, and produced to the same high standards as our books.

We'd very much like to hear from you with your thoughts and ideas for improving what we offer. Please do feel free to email me at sian@globelawandbusiness.com with your views.

Sian O'Neill
Managing director
Globe Law and Business
www.globelawandbusiness.com

www.ingramcontent.com/pod-product-compliance
Ingram Content Group UK Ltd.
Pitfield, Milton Keynes, MK11 3LW, UK
UKHW060150190726
473397UK00005B/49

9 781787 424104